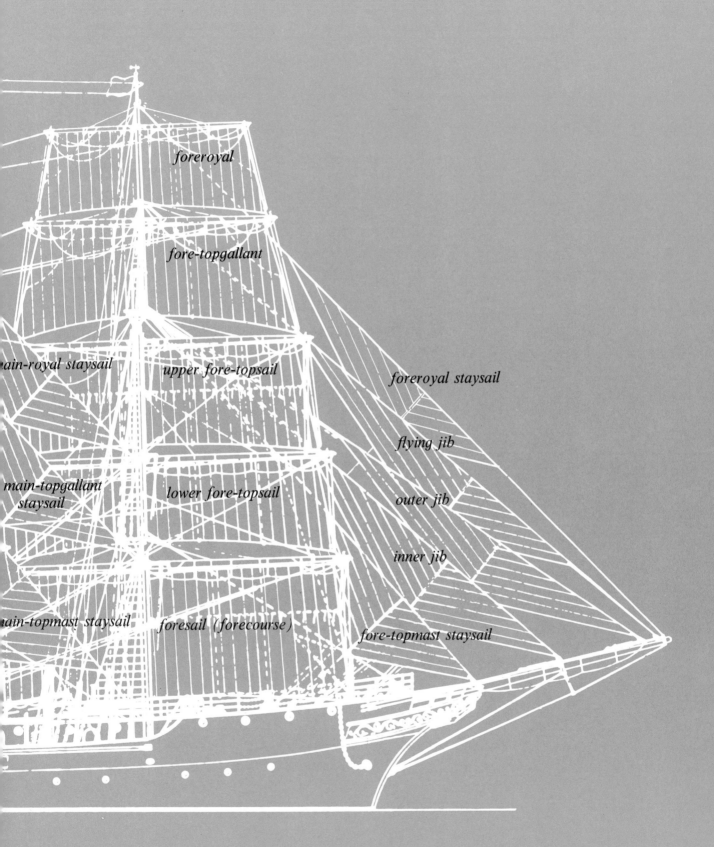

foreroyal

fore-topgallant

main-royal staysail

upper fore-topsail

foreroyal staysail

flying jib

main-topgallant
staysail

lower fore-topsail

outer jib

inner jib

main-topmast staysail

foresail (forecourse)

fore-topmast staysail

 TALL SHIP TO AMERICA

TALL SHIP TO AMERICA

Log of the
CHRISTIAN RADICH

By
KJELL THORSEN

Translated by
LIZANN DISCH

THE TEXAS A&M UNIVERSITY PRESS

College Station and London

*Til min besetning og
våre unge elever*

To my crew and our young cadets

PHOTOGRAPHS: FINN BERGAN

This book is a translation of the Norwegian original «*Christian Radich* – det store Amerikatoktet,» which was copyrighted by J. W. Cappelens Forlag, Oslo, 1977.

Tall Ship to America
is printed
by Grøndahl & Søn A/S,
Norway 1980.

This book is designed
by Bjørg Omholt and Kai Øvre

ISBN (0-89096-096-8)

Admired both from land and water, the ship sails out of Duluth harbor and onto Lake Superior again. PHOTOGRAPH CHARLES CURTIS

The summers of 1975 and 1976 were very eventful and hectic for the square-rigger, the Christian Radich.

In 1975 the school ship participated in the celebration of the 150th anniversary of the Norwegian emigration to America. In 1976 the vessel took part in the big sailing race across the Atlantic, from Plymouth, England, via the Canary Islands and Bermuda to Newport, Rhode Island, in the United States.

In this book I try to impart to the reader the experiences we who manned this proud ship had in the race and during our participation in the U.S.A.'s 200th anniversary celebration that followed.

The unforgettable days in cities on the East Coast and on the Great Lakes have given me and all who were aboard her wonderful memories for the rest of our lives.

It's snowing outside, and the wind is blowing hard. It has been doing this, more or less, all winter. Sleet and snow. Sleet and snow have made life wet and cold.

The ship has been at the yard for four months, ever since we were towed here at the end of October, 1975, after our big American trip. This place is Hommelvik, in the Trondheim Fjord on the Norwegian west coast, and the shipyard is called Trønderverftet A/S – a small but efficient shipyard. They're pretty enterprising, taking on the job of laying a new teak deck on a sailing ship, when few men today have any experience in that kind of work. But with typical Trønder stubbornness and professional competence they have gone to work, and in spite of the bad weather the work has gone according to plan. The ship is completely covered by a roof of tarpaulins, in spite of which rain and snow come in through the openings around the masts and standing rigging. Big heaters, the kind used to dry buildings, keep the newly laid deck dry for caulking.

It has been a tough job. The crew has worked harder than we could reasonably expect them to. Both officers and men have helped pry up old planks and chip rust off the steel plates under the planks before the new deck is laid by the professionals. We had to do it this way in order to have enough money for this big face-lifting job on the ship. The contract with the yard includes the work for which we are using our own crew, to save money. A gift of two million Norwegian kroner was placed at our disposal by the late shipowner, Leif Høegh. We are trying to get as much as we can out of this generous gift which, with a supplementary sum given by our supporting organization, has been stretched to pay for a new deck, a new main engine and auxiliary engines, new panel in the saloon, the mess, and most of the cabins, a new instruction room on the deck, etc. Old electric cables are being replaced; pipes are being repaired by taking out the parts where rust appears to be taking over and putting new pieces in. She'll really be elegant now, 'the Lady'.

'The Lady' is almost forty years old and has a man's name. She was christened *Christian Radich* for the man who gave the money to start construction of a new school training ship for the institution that is now called Østlandets Skoleskib (literally, 'the Eastern District's School Ships Association'). Framnes Shipyards built her in 1937. This yard has shipbuilding traditions extending back into the Viking age. The director of the Main Naval Shipyard in Horten (a city south of Oslo), Captain Chr. Blom, designed her. He was a man with true feeling for line and beauty.

She is a three-masted square-rigger of 676 gross tons; she is 205.0 feet long, has a beam of 32.0 feet, and draws 15.5 feet. Fully rigged, she carries twenty-seven sails, fifteen of which are square sails and the rest staysails. To operate all these sails, 8.5 kilometers (about five miles) of cordage are necessary, and everything is done manually. The hull was constructed of riveted steel plates, and the masts are made of steel tubing. The *Christian Radich's* masts are divided into two parts, the lower mast and the topgallant mast. The three masts are called the foremast, the mainmast, and the mizzenmast.

A lot of young boys have climbed her rigging in the course of these years, set her sails, and thrown up over her railings in the throes of seasickness. And innumerable men have fallen in love with her during the course of these same years.

She became world-renowned as a twenty-year-old, when she was the star of the film *Windjammer*. Seeing her on the screen, with all sails set, gave thousands of people food for their dreams of sailing in tropical waters, with palms and brown girls dressed in next to nothing.

In her belly and on her decks she has carried several thousand young boys who began their seagoing careers in her. She has always been a school training ship; her beauty and grace arouse admiration wherever she goes and have made her homeland famous on foreign shores. Sailors show her the greatest respect upon meeting her at sea or in port. Supertankers and containerships lower their countries' flags in reverence and admiration for her who represents a proud and ancient period in the history of shipping and who carries the flag of a nation that has made a deep and lasting impression in the international world of shipping.

'Christian Radich – Norway's sailing ambassador,' actor/singer Lasse Kolstad sang for the first time in 1974. She was an ambassador most recently in 1975, to the U.S.A., where she visited ports on America's East Coast in conjunction with the 150th anniversary of the Norwegian emigration to the New World. The first emigrants who left their homeland in an organized group to sail across the Atlantic started from Stavanger, on the southwest coast of Norway, on July 4, 1825. To the day, 150 years later, this departure was marked by the *Christian Radich*'s leaving the same city, bound for America. And this time there was great festivity to mark the departure. The city fathers had planned an eventful program, in which the sailing merchantman *Anna* had been 'camouflaged' as the first emigrant ship, the sloop-rigged *Restauration*.

King Olav of Norway visited Stavanger on the occasion of the anniversary, and half an hour before sailing time he and his retinue came aboard to bid us farewell and bon voyage. We were extremely pleased at his interest in the ship and her doings, which emphasized once more our king's understanding of sailing and the sea and wayfaring peoples. The crown prince and crown princess were also on board. The crown prince is the president of the organization Friends of the *Christian Radich,* which supports the vessel financially and in other ways. The Friends are ordinary people, who believe that the craft should be preserved as a school ship and who, by their membership fees and other measures, have made it possible to save her from being laid up and sold. Actor Lasse Kolstad is the enthusiastic chairman of the Friends' organization, and with Norwegian radio's Harald Tusberg and other hard-working people in the administration, we have a good team of supporting players. Liv Ullmann is the organization's 'other figurehead,' a living counterpart of the symbol on the ship's bowsprit. Everyone was there that day.

Our departure day was the crown princess' birthday. She was given flowers on the deck by a very solemn boy from Haugesund.

The Norwegian Minister of Law of the Sea Questions, Jens Evensen, had signed on as supernumerary. He had been and still is one of the ship's most eager partisans. He needed a vacation from his all-consuming work on the division of the seas, and we invited him to come along on a trip to the States that would last for five weeks.

On August 8 we were to be in Miami to do a job for the Norwegian cruise-ship owners who operate from there. One of the shipping companies had helped to finance a set of sails, which was made for us in Hong Kong. The sails were brought by ship to Miami and taken aboard there. The only port of call on the way over was Santa Cruz de Tenerife, where we put in for only a few hours to bunker and take on water before sailing west as fast as we could. The crew was not at all pleased about such a short stay. Understandable, but we were behind schedule, after having been delayed in the Bay of Biscay by southwesterly gales.

American friendliness and hospitality made our visit an experience beyond our wildest dreams. We remember sun-filled days and hectic calls to ports on the East Coast, Norfolk, Alexandria, Baltimore, Philadelphia, and New York. The crew paraded at Virginia Beach, past the copy of the figurehead of the Norwegian bark *Dictator* of Moss, which went down just off the coast there in a storm in March, 1891.

On the return trip, *Christian Radich*'s main engine broke down, south of Nova Scotia. We sailed home without any help from the engines. It took a long time. The winds were very changeable, with hurricanes from the south. We used thirty-two days to England, where we were towed into port at Plymouth. Since it was so late in the year, with pupils who were supposed to go to school, and because of the contract with the shipyard, we were more or less towed all the way to Trondheim, after supplies were taken aboard. The youngsters went their

From the roof of the welding shed at Trønder-verftet in Hommelvik. PHOTOGRAPH: BÅRD GIMNES

Cross section from the fo'c'sle with the new teak deck planks in place. A strong roof has been built over the whole vessel to protect her against the mounds of snow that threatened to break down this shelter when a storm blew up.

respective ways, and the ship was then packed in tarpaulins here at Trønderverftet. While the rebuilding is going on, I am living in an apartment outside the yard area and can see the vessel from my living room window, through the flying snow. She is tugging at her lines, and I like to think that she is eager to get started on new adventures. It looks as though the trip in 1976 will truly be a great and extraordinary adventure.

We are to race across the Atlantic. Race with the really large and famous square-riggers from all over the world. The boys will meet other youth from many countries, sharing common interests. We have been invited to take part in celebrating the U.S.A.'s 200th anniversary. With my memories of last year fresh in mind, I can imagine just how it will be. That is, I can't really – nobody can imagine how it will be on this occasion, when the Americans have promised their guests that they will take part in 'the biggest birthday party ever.'

The planning of our trip has been going on for some time. We were late in saying 'yes, thank you,' because the government was late in guaranteeing the working expenses. The director of Østlandets Skoleskib, Captain Kjeld Backen, has done a monumental job with all of the preparatory correspondence, etc., in conjunction with the planning. There is a lot to think about: the pupils, signing on, medical certificates, repairs, bunkering, currency, invitations from more cities than we could possibly manage to visit . . .

II

88 YOUNG BOYS COME ABOARD

On March 5, 1976, we put out on a trial run with the new machinery. The Veritas classification has been done simultaneously with the repairs and remodeling, and the machinery has been run full out, at the demand of Veritas. I have been given remote control of the main engine from the raised quarterdeck. The new twelve-cylinder G.M. diesel engine responds quickly to the control handle. Reversing goes quickly, and it is a pleasure to run her on engines, too. She does have a few idiosyncrasies, the Lady. You can never be quite sure that she will swing to the same side with her stern every time you ring astern. She is supposed to, theoretically, but once again this is proof that you can't always use common sense in handling women. It sort of depends on her mood. But one thing is certain: you can feel that it feels good to her to be plowing the saltwater again.

We have guests on board – VIPs from Trondheim and the Malvik community, from the board of Østlandets Skoleskib, and from the shipyard, the county, etc. We have been given a berth alongside the pier, free of charge, by the harbormaster, and at the final dinner that evening we make pretty speeches to each other and agree that the vessel has been given the face-lifting she needed.

The next morning we head south. A small tugboat gives us a short push to come around at the mouth of the Nid River. We give a farewell blast on our whistle and chug out the fjord. She is doing a satisfactory nine knots. At Grip we put out to sea, and with Norway on our port we cruise slowly down the coast. At

The boys embark on April 1, 1976. On April 8 we sail out to sea. Here they're waving goodbye to the capital city. PHOTOGRAPH: ØIVIND BARBO

Feie Light we put in. It is early in the morning, and in the shallows at Fedje lies the grounded drilling rig *Deep Sea Driller*. A sad and eerie sight. A wreck is always a dismal sight. One cannot really talk about faded beauty in the wreck of a drilling rig. At any rate, I don't think that a drilling rig has much at all to do with beauty. The stranded rig lies over on her side and reminds us that Nature has once more exacted her fee.

On April 1, eighty-eight boys have come aboard directly from school. At least, most of them have. Some of them have completed the compulsory comprehensive nine-year school the year before, and some of them have been given permission to skip school and take part in the summer's big trip.

What is this bunch like, I wonder. Will they adjust as easily as we are used to their doing? As usual, in admitting new cadets, we ask ourselves these questions. They come from all over the country, but most of them, naturally enough, are from the southeastern districts. We run a training school for young boys who want to be seamen.

All Norwegian boys who want to go to sea before they are seventeen years old must complete a seaman's training course at one of the eight institutions that offer this training. The *Christian Radich* is the only sailing ship playing this role today.

Normally the courses last for three months, but this year we have received

13

At the order 'go aloft' the boys race aloft during sail exercises. They climb in the shrouds – stepping on the ratlines. As can be seen, they hold onto the 'standing' rigging to which the ratlines (the rope steps) are fastened.

PHOTOGRAPH: STIG NÆSS

permission from the Ministry of Education and Ecclesiastical Affairs to keep the same pupils on board throughout the whole trip, which will last for about six months.

Parents have come aboard with their sons, and there is the usual sight of boys who are a bit embarassed when their mothers want to unpack for them in full view of everyone else.

After eight days with these boys, they have begun to find out what is fore and what is aft on the vessel, and we move out from Pier C in Oslo to the cheers and tears of relatives and loved ones. We 'motor-sail' to south England where, based in Tor Bay, we begin intense training with an eye to the sailing race. We let Easter pass by and train on weekends as well as weekdays. Gradually, the boys begin to feel that they are a team. Orders are carried out without any need for yelling, and they set sails, brace yards, furl sails, drop anchor, and weigh anchor as pure routine. You can feel it when the ship has a trained crew. This is a good feeling, and you also feel much safer. The vessel is alive in a different way. If you understand her, she will be your friend. She likes understanding treatment and is unable to resist sweettalk.

On April 23 we take her to dry dock at Falmouth, to Scilley Cox Ltd. She is cleaned up there, and her hull refurbished quite according to the book. Mr. Sutherland and his staff are pleasant hosts, with whom we have become friends. Mrs. Sutherland is a journalist, and she and her readers have a good laugh at the captain's blunder when, in an interview, he says that the ship is in dock 'to clean her bottom'.

Sail job aloft – standing on the footropes, with the backropes for support. Notice that the safety harness is hooked onto the backrope.

PHOTOGRAPH: HARALD TUSBERG

PHOTOGRAPH: STIG NÆSS

Painting the bottom before the race. The vessel was docked at Scilley Cox in Falmouth in April, 1976. This port, rich in tradition, has seen many a sailing ship in her day.

PHOTOGRAPH: TROND O. RØED

The mainmast's port rigging and rigging screws, with pinrail underneath.

PHOTOGRAPH: KAI ØVRE

Milbay Dock in Plymouth is teeming with life. I am convinced that this has also been the case many times before, during its history, but it must be seldom that this dock has seen so many ships and boats bound for America at one time. *Tovarishch*, formerly *Gorch Fock*, of the Soviet Union, is lying there. *Dar Pormorza* of Poland lies just outside the dock gate and is not able to enjoy being able to disregard high and low tides. *Kruzenshtern* from the Soviet Union lies at anchor out in the bay. A small brigantine by the name of *Phoenix*, registered in Ireland, lies alongside two beautiful Baltic Sea schooners.

The fleet is divided into classes, and Class A includes all square-riggers over 150 gross tonnage. *Phoenix* just falls into Class A, with her 151 tons. The smaller vessels have been divided into classes B and C.

The tall ship race, as it is called – the sailing race in which the square-riggers are the main actors – is arranged every other year by the Sail Training Association (STA), which has its headquarters in London. School ships from all over the world are invited to take part, and the fundamental idea behind the whole arrangement is to give young people from as many countries as possible an opportunity to meet in peaceful competition, become acquainted with each other, and learn to understand and accept other countries' customs, in the hope that these arrangements can, in the long run, contribute to creating international understanding and a better world.

Mainmast's base with mizzen braces, topping lifts, and mainmast's sheets coiled.
PHOTOGRAPH: HARALD TUSBERG

I meet Nick for the first time at Milbay Dock. I will come to know him as an adventurer, a bohemian, and a really good guy. He is not obtrusively rich in this world's material objects, but he owns and loves an old Baltic Sea vessel, rigged as a topsail schooner. Nick was born and grew up on the Dutch island of Texel, but I think that he gave in to his hankering for adventure pretty early.

He comes aboard on a sunny day. 'Can I see the captain?' I hear from a voice bellowing out in the passageway. Into the saloon comes a tall, skinny man with a huge beard, sideburns, and clothes that have undoubtedly seen their best days. I ask him to sit down. We are just having a coffee break, and before he tells me his errand I ask if he wants a cup of coffee, or a drink perhaps? The man does not seem to be the type who lacks for words, but where the important things of life are concerned he evidently wastes few words. 'Whiskey,' he answers. His name is Nicholas Decker, and he is a Dutchman. On the way into Plymouth we had sailed past a black-painted vessel, which we had swung in to and greeted. The ship was called *Artemis*. At high tide the next day she had come in and been given a berth at the coal dock. It was Nick's ship. Now Nick was coming to us to ask for permission to come alongside the *Christian Radich*.

'You see, Captain, these bloody Englishmen are ruining my new sails.' Oh? My questioning look produces a hint of irritation in Nick. All of the harbor must have realized that the coal dust from the pier has dirtied his sails! This has escaped my notice, but so as not to irritate our guest I keep quiet about this. 'You see, Captain Decker, my port side was painted yesterday, but if you are careful and have clean fenders, you can come alongside after lunch.' I can almost read his thoughts: 'New paint, clean fenders, does this guy think I'm an idiot?' 'Thank you, Captain.' Nick empties his glass and lets me know that now he is busy and cannot, unfortunately, bestow his presence upon me any longer. When important things are to be done, there evidently is no nonsense about Captain Decker.

I take a walk up to the regatta office, which is housed in a small brick building on the dock. Nice people, these men who run the Sail Training Association. Voluntary work, no pay. Idealists still exist. Programs and information of all kinds that may be of interest to the participants are lying ready in envelopes and are turned over in return for a receipt by STA's lovely secretary, Leslie. Each of the large vessels has been assigned its liaison officer, and I invite ours to lunch.

Yardarm with the sail clewed up before it is furled. The sail's roping is hauled up with clewlines and buntlines. PHOTOGRAPH HARALD TUSBERG

Behind some warehouses Chief Officer Jan Fjeld-Hansen is giving marching instruction to the cadets. They are to parade down Broadway when the time comes, and we have to train them at every opportunity. These pups have never marched before, it seems. When one has grown up in uniform, it seems slightly odd that some people always connect marching with an ambling gait. I meet Jan's desperate but still optimistic glance.

Nick evidently eats lunch at different times than we do, because, when I come on board again, *Artemis* is already lying alongside. First Mate Fred Hegerstrøm, who is also the radio officer, is already at work repairing Nick's radio. I am invited on board by Nick. He tells me a little about himself. Ordinarily he earns his daily bread by selling antiques. He runs a floating antique shop. He travels around France, buying up old objects, takes them on board, and sells them from the ship in different ports. Because of this, his hold is now completely empty. He is not doing business during this race. He has signed on (for their keep) a young crew, as the participation rules stipulate, and his plan is to make the ship's name famous. He appears to have some sort of deal going with a French wine firm. Is it possible to get the Americans to like wine brought from France on a sailing ship? It would, of course, be somewhat more expensive...

Nick's laughter booms out, coming from deep down in his stomach. He laughs when he tells about his radio equipment. 'You see, Captain, I like to be by myself at sea, but in order to take part in this bloody sailing race I had to get a radio. I have to keep to my style, so I bought... well, I'd call it an antique radio. Old as the devil...' Nick spices his language with strong oaths. Fred gets his radio to work, at least as far as our receiver, ten meters away. Nick is satisfied.

After lunch I go up to the Norwegian Consulate, which is nearby. On the dock a number of photographers are busy taking pictures of the fleet in the harbor, and one of them grins happily as he takes a picture of a cadet who is washing the figurehead, 'Christina'. He shoots just as the boy is lying in the safety net, lovingly washing Christina's breasts.

At the consulate I am given advance wages for the crew and some mail from Norway. I also take care of formalities in connection with sending home a couple of the cadets, who unfortunately cannot adjust to life on board. It's too bad; think of the experiences they'll miss. We start in two days, so it's too late to even think about replacements from Norway. Two days until we start! My first start in a sailing race with square-riggers. The eggs have already been laid for a couple of butterflies in my stomach.

A lot of boys are needed in the rigging of a square-rigger – 'one hand for the ship and one hand for yourself.' PHOTOGRAPH: LYNETTE MILLER

At the start from Bermuda, on the last leg to Newport. On the right, the 'Gorch Foch', in the middle the 'Libertad' with green sails, behind her, the 'Christian Radich', and, far left, the 'Kruzenshtern'.

III

THE RACE
TO TENERIFE

Mainmast's top and topgallant crosstrees.
PHOTOGRAPH: KAI ØVRE

Sunday, May 2, is the big day. The dock gate was opened and we got out last evening. We have been lying at anchor, at the ready, all night. At nine o'clock the dock gates open again, and here they come, the B and C classes. At twelve o'clock we are supposed to start. The starting line is marked by two vessels out in Plymouth Bay. The pleasure craft are out, of course, to watch the event. A southwesterly moderate breeze is blowing. This means a close-hauled start and beating out in the Channel. Try to come up to the windward mark! Everyone wants to do this, of course, and since this is my first start I stay relatively modestly in the background, not wanting to risk jumping the gun. They are not exactly as maneuverable as dinghies, these large ships, and it can take hours to get back in position to restart.

We start on a southeasterly course, and to windward I have *Dar Pormorza* and *Kruzenshtern*. *Tovarishch* and *Phoenix* come up from leeward aft. The *Dar Pormorza* takes the lead in a beautiful start. We are neck and neck with *Kruzenshtern* and clawing to windward. The wind freshens a little, but the direction stays the same for the moment. How long are we going to stay on course for the French coast? OK, here's your chance, boy – this is called 'using tactics'. I wonder what the other captains are figuring out. We are all trying to read each other's minds.

I decide to keep on course closer to the French coast. It looks as though Schneider on the *Kruzenshtern* has decided to do the same, because when the sun sets in the sea, over there in the west, *Dar Pormorza* and the *Tovarishch* have turned and are sailing in towards the English coast again.

I know a couple of these men who captain the big ships very slightly. Jurkiewich of the *Dar Pormorza* is one of the sea's noblemen. Thirty-two years on the same ship has made him a kind of institution for the Poles. He is to go ashore in March, next year. Then young Ted, who is along on the trip to learn the tricks of the trade from the old man, will take over. Schneider of the *Kruzenshtern* I have met at the Royal West Yacht Club's farewell party for the participants. I still haven't met Vandenko of the *Tovarishch*.

Usually there is a lot of traffic here in the Channel, but as the darkness of the night erases the horizon, only the lanterns on *Kruzenshtern* are visible on the sea.

Last year I had been very impressed with our new radar, when we recorded the echo of Pico de Teyde on Tenerife, on maximum range, sixty-four nautical miles. We are now lying about forty miles off Teyde, but still nothing is to be seen on the screen, nor are there any other echoes.

We are almost ten days out of Plymouth. At the start we stood westward to gain height on Biscay. Every twenty-four hours we have reported our position to the schooner *Sir Winston Churchill,* which is the communications ship, and from there a collective report has been sent out every morning to the whole fleet. In that way we can plot each other, and it is exciting to see how the race has been developing.

All of the others in our class have sailed closer to land. They have 'cut corners' around D'Ouessant and have put south through Biscay. To really fix things, the *Christian Radich* has had twelve hours with thick fog and complete calm. It is a local fog, because ten to twelve miles west and east of us we hear by radio that there are favorable winds. It's in situations like this that your smile muscles refuse to react naturally. You become irritable and difficult to talk to. I have noticed that the crew does not come to me on unnecessary errands. The three largest ships gradually pull away from us. We do, of course, have a handicap factor (time used is multiplied by a handicap factor, which is calculated on the basis of the ship's length of waterline, her sail area, shape of propeller, etc.). This will help us some, but at the moment it looks to me as if we are going to reach the finish line at Santa Cruz as number four. Nothing to do about that. They are evidently better sailors than we are. *Tovarishch* is clearly number one, then *Kruzenshtern* is in second place, and then there is the *Dar Pormorza,* which we still have a minute chance to beat.

A few days ago we were ahead of *Kruzenshtern* for awhile, but then she made a few formidable leaps and took a clear lead. It's amazing how the winds can vary in strength locally. This morning we have heard that *Tovarishch* has crossed the finish line and is lying in port. The *Kruzenshtern* is expected a few hours later. Oh well, we'll have to try to do better on the next leg – to Bermuda.

Finally, something that looks like land takes on contours on the radar screen. Yes, it is the northeast point of Tenerife, just barely thirty miles away. The radar is definitely not what it once was.

The wind is west by south. I wonder what it's like, closer to the coast. Way in, it will be almost completely calm, of course, with possibilities of winds dropping off the high mountains. We choose to race down along the east side of the island, a few miles from land. Not too far, because then we risk having to tack to the mark, which is located eight nautical miles southeast of the harbor entrance.

There is a good wind all the way, until just abreast of the island. Then it stops almost completely. We see the lanterns of – yes, it must be a B-class or C-class boat close to the shore – and we are clearly pulling away from him. The wind changes direction, and we are close-hauled on a starboard tack. Will this be enough to get us in to the finish line? This is exciting! Slowly, slowly we move, until dawn. Then the wind freshens considerably – so much so that the vessel ships water in the washports on the main deck, as the ship is tossed from side to side. This is the measurement we ordinarily use to show that now we have to strike the royals (which means that we have to lower and furl the sails), but not now, oh, no! Hang on a little longer! Claw to windward in the gusts, men! We need every inch now! Tensely we watch the radar. The finish line is not marked with anything but the given bearing and distance from the southern pier head at the harbor entrance to Santa Cruz. It's enough – it's enough with just one-half nautical mile, just 1.000 short yards, 3.000 feet. We can even let ourselves fall off a little in the final minutes to increase our speed. 'There!' our Swedish junior second mate, Henrik Wrede, yells from the bearing platform. We cross the finish line at 0733 hours and some seconds (35) on May 13.

'Man stations, ready to go aloft.' The boys are ready in the windward lower shrouds immediately. The sails are lowered, and the boys race up the rigging to furl them. The job is done quickly, the boys inspired by the thought of an exciting liberty in Santa Cruz. The *Dar Pormorza* is lying south of us and running engines with furled sails towards the harbor entrance. Has she just arrived, just before us? Then maybe we have a chance at third place? I call Jurkiewich on the radio. Nope, they crossed the finishing line late last evening and have just waited until it was light to put in.

The pilot embarks. A big man for a Spaniard. He talks with machine-gun rapidity into the walkie-talkie. He puts on a lot of speed to go in. I ask him to slow down. Tugboats are making fast forward and aft. The pilot gives his orders curtly. The tugs set off at full speed, and our new nylon ropes are stretched to the breaking point. I don't like this. If one of them snaps, the vessel will put on speed and ram something or other. The pilot is ordered to slow down. He pretends that he doesn't understand a thing. I have to speak harshly to him. He looks at me with his wounded cocker spaniel look and says, 'You must trust me, Captain.' At last we are alongside the pier, safe and sound – in spite of the pilot. On the pier the consul and vice-consul, with their families, are waiting to welcome us. We had met them very briefly last year when we put in to bunker.

All through the day they come in, the B- and C-classes. That is, the regatta machines – the modern speed-sailers – have, of course, been lying in port for a long time. The fishing harbor in the north of the basin is crammed full of these racers. The piers we are lying alongside gradually fill up with the schooners, mostly the Baltic Sea workhorses. The *Regina Maris* also comes in. She was rebuilt at Høyvold's Verksted in my hometown of Kristiansand years ago. *Lindo* and *Gefion* are beautiful ships, remodeled for cruise traffic, and rebuilt with piety in order to retain the old style. After official duties are completed, I wander

View from the fore-topgallant crosstrees. We see the main-topmast staysail (the fore-and-aft sail in the foreground) and lower main-topsail.
PHOTOGRAPH: HARALD TUSBERG

along the piers. For someone who loves boats or who, perhaps, is boat-mad, it is sheer joy to see and smell the atmosphere around these ships. The *Gladan,* which is representing the Swedish Navy, has sailed well and has already taken down the foremast, which had broken during the race. A new mast will arrive from Sweden in a couple of days.

Tourists from many countries, of all ages and sizes, stream into Santa Cruz to see this rare sight. I take a few pictures for an album I plan to make, fill the whole camera lens with masts and yards. It is just beautiful. It's such a shame that a picture cannot capture the feeling, the smells, the sounds, and everything that helps to create the illusion of a time when people let the winds blow them across the seas.

We go through the program for our stay in Santa Cruz. The cadets are to see the island by bus, and of course they will be taken on the traditional trip for tourists, to Pico de Teyde, the highest mountain in the Canary Islands, 3.716 meters high. This is a good landmark when visibility is good. The peak is covered with snow all year round and is a favorite spot for many Scandinavians who go to the Canary Islands to find sun and warmth – and why that is, I don't know!

The youngsters are also to take part in some sports competitions. In addition, we are to have a two-day minicruise out from the harbor, with an exchange of pupils. The STA is expending a lot of effort to make this popular. Enthusiastic Lieutenant Colonel James Myatt is running around to all the ships and making lists of those who are to be 'exchanged,' so that they know exactly where everyone is. The Soviets were a bit skeptical to begin with, but they have finally agreed to the program.

The plan is to sail out in the morning, cast anchor in the evening, all together, let the boys run ashore to a grill party and self-produced fun on the beach at Los Cristianos, on the southern part of the island, and return to Santa Cruz the next day.

Before we leave on the minicruise, we are going to celebrate May Seventeenth (Norwegian Constitution Day). Not too many people in the fleet know about our national holiday, perhaps, aside from the Swedes, but a slight hint to STA starts the rumors flying. The day arrives, and most of the fleet dress ship in Norway's honor. This is quite a sight!

We celebrate the day with a half-holiday for the boys and chicken for dinner. The next day we have a reception on board for some of the resident Norwegian families, with Consul Lindberg at their head. Through Lindberg, I have invited one of the heroes of my boyhood and the war, Jan Baalsrud, the 'man with nine lives.' To my great pleasure, he comes. He is a nice guy, who has now settled down here in a climate better suited to his health. He is a farmer up in the mountains. Rumors about his products have spread, and he has no difficulty in selling them. Men like Baalsrud command our deepest respect.

On May 19 we embark on our minicruise. James Myatt has been successful in his efforts. Almost the whole fleet sails to Los Cristianos. The original plan was a foray on Gran Canaria, but the local Tenerife authorities have insisted that a harbor on that island be used. They want currency spent on their island as compensation for all the work and money that has been put into the arrangements in Santa Cruz. So, Los Cristianos it is. A small, sleepy village, completely devoid of any possibilities for spending money. Besides which, boys from a sailing fleet are not particularly fat in the pocket – quite the contrary, in fact. The STA staff wanted to go along on this ship, and we had no objections to their choosing the *Christian Radich.* They bring along the general who is chief of the Spanish Army units on the island. He is a passionate sailor and has expressed a wish to sail with a square-rigger.

The wind is fine and northerly. We want to put to parallel with *Tovarishch* to study her sails and compare them with ours. I have the feeling that our sails are

An 'eyelet hole' or 'cringle' in the sail's clew (the lower corner), to which the clewlines, tacks, and sheets are shackled. On the new dacron sails this construction has been slightly changed.

PHOTOGRAPH: HARALD TUSBERG

The barquentine 'Regina Maris', rebuilt in Kristiansand a long time ago, now sailing under the U.S. flag. PHOTOGRAPH FROM: TALL SHIPS

One of many fine sea cadets – this one from the 1975 group. PHOTOGRAPH: WILLIAM RHYINS

Aloft in the mainsail's lower port shrouds.

too flat. There is no real give in them. The old sailmakers sewed flat sails. The hempen canvas stretches and gives after the sails have been used for awhile. The modern synthetic materials don't do this. Our sails, sewed of American dacron, won't stretch, and the shape of the sails stays the same. I want to look at the *Tovarishch,* because she obviously sails much faster than other ships. A flaw in our pleasure in the race was when a protest for cheating was registered. This resulted in a closed meeting of the regatta committee. The protest was not followed up because of a lack of evidence. The protest came from a Class-C boat, which claimed that the *Tovarishch* had used her engine.

We sail with a wind on the starboard beam. We are actually pulling away from *Tovarishch.* She also has new sails, made of synthetic materials. They look just as flat as ours do.

Our experience is that the *Christian Radich* sails faster in this light wind than her larger competitors. In stronger winds, however, with choppier seas, the larger ships with a long waterline will sail faster.

We are to have pork chops and fresh salad for lunch. I seat the senior member from STA, Lord Bernham, at my table on the port side of the saloon. He sits with his back to starboard. The ship lists a little. We can feel that the wind is freshening. Just as we have been served with the table's delicacies, there is a gust of wind that forces the vessel to heel to starboard. The lord almost tips backwards on his chair, but grabs hold of the table. The table is bolted to the deck, but the lord is not strong enough to hold on. He loses hold, and the chair, with him sitting on it, slides down to the lee side and hits the furniture. Most of what was on the table follows the lord across the deck – pork chops, salad, bread, cups, glasses, everything slides along. Fortunately I do not give way to my impulse to exclaim 'Good Lord!'

I go on deck to see how the weather is. It certainly has freshened! Naturally enough, *Tovarishch* has come up to us. She is a beautiful sight as she skims along, doing twelve to fourteen knots. The next leg of the race should prove exciting. I hope we will lose the despondent feeling we had in Santa Cruz. To my astonishment we have beaten the *Dar Pormorza.* We had figured our handicap factor wrong.

The foray on Los Cristianos is as successful as could be. The boys are ashore with their colleagues from other ships and boats – fraternization among the nations as ever was!

We sail back to Santa Cruz, or rather, we use our engine. It would take too much time to tack in that hard head wind and current. It is late evening before we put in to the dock again. There is a different harbor pilot this time, and he takes it much easier than the first one did.

When a light breeze fills the sails, the buntlines and doublings of the canvas can be seen where they press against the sail.
PHOTOGRAPH: HARALD TUSBERG

Evening in the trade-wind belt. There is a fantastic play of color of the sun, sea, and clouds in the clear air. PHOTOGRAPH: FINN BERGAN

IV

THE NORTHEAST TRADE WIND – THAT DISAPPEARED

The rudder trunk with the wheel and grating.
PHOTOGRAPH: KAI ØVRE

On May 23, at lunchtime, the tugs arrive to take the fleet out of the harbor. The A-Class has been expanded by two large ships. The topsail schooner, the four-master *Juan Sebastian de Elcano,* belonging to the Spanish Navy, and the three-masted bark *Sargres,* from Portugal, are the newcomers, along with the much smaller *Regina Maris,* which now flies the American flag.

At four o'clock in the afternoon we are to start on the next stretch across the Atlantic. Bermuda is the first stop, 2.500 nautical miles to the west. We are to start outside the harbor inlet, so that as many people as possible will be able to see the sight from shore. In addition, everything that can float in the way of pleasure craft and commercial boats is out, full of passengers. Two smaller boats, which mark the starting line, have a balloon on a long rope, so that they can be identified more easily among the many rushing around in all directions in the starting area. The wind is northerly and fine for a downwind start.

The *Christian Radich* crosses the starting line more or less together with *Dar Pormorza,* the *Juan Sebastian de Elcano,* and the *Regina Maris.* Both of the Soviet vessels and the *Sargres* are lying somewhat astern on the port. The *Kruzenshtern* was unlucky and sailed on the wrong side of the starting boat. Having to go back and restart will cost her several hours.

Last year, when we sailed on what was generally this same route, I found that the wind was unstable close to the islands Gomera and Hierro. It is necessary to find the normally steady and sure northeast trade wind. This has always been used by westbound sailing ships. For this reason I have chosen to sail southward to about twenty-seven degrees north before we start west. The *Dar Pormorza* and both of the Soviets are sailing very close to the islands where I believe the wind conditions to be unfavorable. The captains on those ships obviously think otherwise, and they are right. The head winds I assumed they would have are absent, instead of which they have favorable winds westward.

The boys are looking forward to a few weeks at sea. Ten days in Santa Cruz is a bit long. Even though the country and the people were unknown and exciting, to begin with, and fraternization with the other crews was successful, they are longing to go to sea again. The 'deep blue sea' exerts a powerful attraction, and, when it keeps a temperature of slightly more than twenty-five degrees centigrade and the sun is large and warm and almost in zenith, it's good to be alive. Everyday wear, in general, is bathing trunks, even during the night. We have no artificial ventilation in the form of fans or air-conditioning on board. Because of this it gets hot in the cabins and on the mess decks. The portholes on the sides of the ship on the lower deck (the mess deck) are, of course, closed while at sea, and this does not improve matters at all. It does a frozen Northerner's body good to sweat. Last winter, with its snowstorms and filthy weather for months up there in Hommelvik, is still remembered. We hope that our friends up there have a summer that makes up for that winter.

During the first few days of this leg, the *Dar Pormorza* has done very well. We haven't done so badly, either – number two! It is very exciting to follow the daily positions of the fleet. Captain Collis, on board the *Sir Winston Churchill,* the man with the monocle, sends out a report on positions every day in his very cultivated English. After a few days, both of the Soviets come up. They sail up to the fore in front of the Pole and us. *Tovarishch* plows ahead several miles per day. She is somewhat north of us and farther west. The *Kruzenshtern* is south of us. Gradually we get less and less wind. We are obviously in a calm belt.

More than a week out of Santa Cruz the trade wind, the steady, dependable wind that is created by equatorial masses of air rising straight up and air from the south and north streaming in to fill up the 'vacuum' that results, is a thing of the past. Because of the earth's rotation, the direction of the wind that streams in from the north is northeasterly, and similarly, there is a southeasterly wind south of the equator. We are completely becalmed. Absolutely still. Once in a great while, as happens in the Inner Oslofjord on a Sunday morning, there is a slight breath of wind, which just barely ruffles the surface of the water. All wind must be utilized, and we haul around as the wind, what little there is, blows all over the compass card.

Aside from this matter of the wind, which is, of course, the same for everyone, or at least almost the same, our life out here is marvelous. Every day the chief officer and I give the boys physical training. It feels good, afterwards, to get under the saltwater shower on the deck to cool off. We also give them some instruction. This is usually done on the deck, since the mess decks are sheer ovens. We have brought along a few films for entertainment, and with the after bulkhead of the forward deckhouse as the screen, movies are shown under the starry canopy of the tropical skies. The boys 'take their seats' lying around on the hard deck during the performance.

We haven't bunkered since Plymouth. I calculated on a trip of fourteen to sixteen days from Santa Cruz to Bermuda. We only need fuel for the auxiliary machinery and some for the main engine in and out of harbors.

It is now quite obvious that we are not going to reach the finish line by the appointed time. The time the program gives as 'Endex' is June 13, at 1900 hours (7:00 P.M.) local time. In order to save fuel we find it necessary to stop the auxiliary engine for part of the day. Our Lister auxiliary engine uses 250 liters of diesel oil per day. I have six tons left, and I know that we will have to use the engine from the thirteenth until we reach Bermuda. When the auxiliary engine is stopped, the gyro stops, the main radio transmitter and receiver, the freezer, the sanitary pumps, etc., all of these also stop working. And the lighting, of course. We bring out our kerosene lanterns and bat-wing lamps and the kerosene lamp for the compass. We fill large casks with water, in advance, to flush out the toilets. We have a youngster on watch who sees to it that the toilets in the fore are properly flushed. 'Head watch,' the boys call it.

It is an odd experience to stop the auxiliary engine. No sounds from the exhaust pipe, only kerosene lamps, kerosene lanterns. Silence. The creaking of the rigging is heard above all other sounds. Only boys' voices from the fo'c'sle reveal that there are people on board. It is difficult to settle down to sleep. Every minute must be experienced to the utmost. It may be a long time before we sail under conditions like these again. One of the sea's many faces.

The *Sir Winston Churchill* has now come so far west that she has difficulties communicating with the whole fleet. We are spread out over a thousand miles, and many of the radios are fairly weak. The race committee looks around for another suitable vessel, which can take over. The *Christian Radich* is asked to do this. Fred Hegerstrøm must now take on this job, besides his regular watches. It takes a lot of time, but I think that he also feels quite complimented at being asked to do the job. He has made overview charts with all the names of the participating vessels, the class divisions, etc. It works very well. Our strong radio comes into its own.

Time passes by, and we drift slowly, so slowly westward. Some days we reach a twenty-four-hour run of sixty miles, and this is wonderful. Until we hear that others have sailed twice as far.

We discuss by radio whether there is any sense in continuing until June 13. Several of the smaller boats have had difficulties with fuel for their power plants and their water supply. They also have crew members who are supposed to fly home from Bermuda, with charter-planes ordered in advance. All of the captains we can reach by radio agree that we should break off, using our final positions in calculating our placing, and get to Bermuda as fast as we can by using our machinery. We offer to tow the smaller vessels that do not have enough fuel. We have made direct radio contact with the STA office, Bermuda. Our suggestion to break off falls on deaf ears. No arguments help. 'Stick to the rules!' They will not give in, by damn!

In order to 'let off a little steam' I write a poem, which I hope to find an

She can be difficult to steer, and then it's good to have four hands on the spokes.
PHOTOGRAPH: T. RØNNIG

As though it had been dipped in dye.
PHOTOGRAPH: FINN BERGAN

opportunity to read for STA. It's about this part of the race, seen through the eyes of a sixteen-year-old Norwegian:

One Sunday at the end of May
A masted fleet stood out to sail,
To cross the waves for STA
The oceans wide with storms and hail.

We sailed one week and all was well.
The Trade Winds blew to satisfaction.
Smooth sea, sunshine, a little swell.
But wind came from the wrong direction.

The wind died out, we got nowhere,
Bermuda Isles are far from here.
The captain said, 'Oh, what a show,
We bloody well can start to row.'

Oh, Lord, I thought, he's quite insane.
To row that far is all in vain.
I ran to hide, I was afraid.
Where could I go, yes, to the head.

The captain's mad, I heard the rumor.
He's lost his normal sense of humor.
I heard them whisper 'See his face!
I'm sure he's going to end this race!'

I sat there many, many days
Before I dared to show my face.
I tiptoed to the bridge to see
What happened there, oh, pity me!

The captain – his mind gone at last?
He stood there, redfaced, scratched the mast.
But still no change, the wind was dead.
Then, captain's hat on helmsman's head.

That used to work in a bygone day,
Before sailing for the STA.
But now the gods of waves and weather,
Did not send wind to blow a feather.

The fleet was fed up. On the air
By radio you heard them swear.
The captains' language to each other
Would never win favor with any mother.

The race was off on 13th June.
It ended with the engine's tune.
The quiet sea we had to spoil
With smoke and smell of diesel oil.

On June 15 we see Bermuda on the radar. Most of us have never been here before, and, as usual, our curiosity has reached the great heights it achieves when we call at unknown ports. Bermuda is not just one island. There are 350 in

all. Twenty of them are inhabited, and most of them are linked together with bridges. They are coral islands, the world's most northerly.

The low islands are poor radar land. We are to put into Saint George to bunker and take on water. Several of the smaller ships are already lying there. By radio we receive orders to anchor northeast of the entrance at Five Fathom Hole and not to put in to port until early the next morning. Gradually, several of the other large ships cast anchor around us.

In earlier days Bermuda was known for her cedar trees. Many ships were built here of this kind of wood, which is very resistant to rot. The cedar forests on Bermuda have long since disappeared. Through binoculars it looks as though the rose bushes by the many beautiful homes are the tallest vegetation on the islands. Human beings have certainly fixed things for themselves. The Norwegians exported all their good oak wood from the southern coast and Jæren. The large oak stands are also gone.

A well-built, small, dark-skinned pilot comes out to take us in to the bunker station. The bunker station is an ordinary pier, and we have to get our fuel from a tank truck. We tie up just ahead of a passenger ship, where curious tourists hang over the rail and look at this strange vessel with yards and masts. I have a faint suspicion that those who do not have any feeling for sailing ships and beauty just shake their heads and go into the bar to get a drink.

Mr. Butterfield, our consul in Hamilton, the island's capital, is ill. He has gotten lumbago, but his efficient wife jumps into her car and drives to Saint George. She arranges matters with the ship's chandler and the bunker people and arranges for money for wages, mail, the customs, all those things that have to be done when a ship puts into port. We invite her to lunch. And not just out of courtesy.

Furling the spanker.

Tugs-of-war between the boys and the officers is a popular pastime during lazy days in the trades.
PHOTOGRAPH: ØIVIND BARBO

By late afternoon of the next day we have finished our bunkering and our four water tanks have been filled to the top. It is necessary, as usual, to have a pilot, and one of these local coastal pathfinders comes aboard. He takes us into Hamilton Harbor, where we cast anchor with the largest fleet of school ships the world has ever seen – sixteen square-riggers, of which most are more than 2.000 tons. The only one missing is Japan's *Nippon Maru*. The smaller vessels are moored, stern to the wharf, most of them outside the Princess Hotel. The STA has its office in an annex there.

The harbor area is surrounded by beautiful houses with luxuriant gardens. In the semitropical climate on this remarkable island, 700 nautical miles off the coast of North America, there appears to be very good soil. I am no botanical expert, who would know the names of all of these large, multicolored blooms, but it certainly is lovely.

The hands to go on liberty fall in up on the main deck for inspection before they enter the boat. Young, expectant faces. After almost a month at sea it will feel good to stretch their legs. What is Bermuda like, do you suppose?

Bermuda has gone all out on tourism. It is a holiday paradise, which has long since been discovered by relatively well-to-do people. The prices reflect this. Almost as expensive as at home.

The authorities have been sensible enough to prohibit large cars for private transport. Small roads hum almost constantly with mopeds, which everyone appears to have.

Young people from the sailing fleet, most of them in uniform, are seen all over the place, and young girls are given many an undisguised, admiring glance.

At the race office they welcome us to port. The only ship that still has not been heard of is *Artemis,* with my friend Nick aboard. His antique radio is too poor. A week previously we had heard that he had very little fuel and water. At that time we had asked STA to try to find *Artemis* by plane. I had indicated that perhaps planes should be sent out from the Azores. This was probably just disregarded. Nick has since been in contact with a Greek vessel to get diesel oil for his engines. We know too that he was personally on board the Greek. For some reason he did not get his fuel. It would have been interesting to have been a fly on the wall during that conversation.

Eventually I meet the captains of the large ships that have joined the fleet. Captain Hansen of the school-ship *Danmark* is a veteran of sailing ships. This ship spends half the year in Caribbean waters. Von Stakkelberg on the *Gorch Fock* is a man who does not hide his light under a bushel. He is full of humor and a very nice guy. They are all very nice, each in his own way. They are individualists with their own special features. Captain Martin, of the *Esmeralda*, from Chile, is an elegant chap; he has lost his right arm below the elbow. Now he wears a real steel claw, just like those the old pirates had in our boyhood fantasies. *Esmeralda* is the sistership of *Juan Sebastian de Elcano*. I also meet Captain Oleg Vandenko of the *Tovarishch*. He was one hour from the finish line when the race was called off. Again the Soviets came in as number one and two. Rumors are rife, as they were in Santa Cruz. Again the newspapers are speculating openly. It is a fact that the two Soviet vessels moved very swiftly during the last week of the race, while the rest of the fleet has more or less been lying becalmed. Again I receive the third prize, awarded by the governor.

Along with three other captains, I am invited on board the *Tovarishch,* and in a closed meeting we square things up as well as we can.

The day of the start of the big race is fast approaching. All sixteen of the Class-A ships are to start at the same time. Never can there have been such a mass start of large sailing ships before. We have studied the program and have

Serving on the shrouds to prevent chafing of the sails.   PHOTOGRAPH: KAI ØVRE

V

THE BATTLE OF BERMUDA

The square-rigger 'Libertad' from Chile crosses the track and is on a collision course with the four-masted topsail-schooner 'Juan Sebastian de Elcano' of Spain.

PHOTOGRAPH: BERMUDA NEWS SERVICE

been informed that the starting line is 1.2 nautical miles wide. Everything is relative to something else in this world – 1.2 nautical miles is a long way to swim, but as the starting line for so many large ships it seems extremely short.

At the captains' meeting on June 19 the leg from Santa Cruz to Bermuda is discussed first of all. The mood of the members is one of dissatisfaction. Poor wind conditions were not anyone's fault, but we think that the whole affair could have been called off at a much earlier point. Some of the ships have had very little time ashore before they had to be ready for the next start. I have the poem I had written while at sea in my pocket. In an effort to lighten the atmosphere I stand up and read it. Fortunately, this helps.

On the initiative of the *Danmark* we discuss the use of engines before a start with the race committee. According to valid rules, the ships can use their engines 'for safety' up to five minutes prior to the starting gun. If the propeller is used after this time, time is added to the elapsed time. After a vote taken among the captains, where the race committee would have had a sheer majority, it is decided that, for this special start, the propeller can be used up to the time of the starting gun if necessary, without any time added. We think that this is a great improvement, since we all have to start at the same time on such a short line.

At eight o'clock on Sunday, June 20, the fleet begins to move. In the quiet harbor, where the morning breeze has barely begun to make itself felt, voices can be heard in the distance from the other ships. Anchor chains begin to rattle. The pilot boat dashes around, delivering one pilot to each ship. We get the same man who had taken us into Saint George.

We leave the harbor according to the departure plan. One by one the great ships ease out of the idyllic harbor. Wonder if I'll ever come back here. Maybe in

The collision is a fact, and the 'Juan Sebastian's bowsprit rips the sails and rigging on the 'Libertad'.

my own boat. There comes a black ship, chugging into harbor. Nick, on *Artemis*. He waves as he passes. 'Not too much time, Nick, before the next start.' Everything appears to be well on board, and we bid our adieus, until we see each other in Newport.

We use our engine out the buoy-marked channel, northward to the starting area. Again, everything that can float, in the way of pleasure craft, has come out to watch. The starting line is marked by two vessels. The wind stands from the south-southeast, and the line is laid somewhat across the direction of the wind. The marker vessels are anchored in position; it is the depth conditions that have determined such a short starting line. The relatively shallow waters outside the reef on the north side of the island suddenly deepen to Atlantic Ocean depths.

The farthest mark vessel is H.M.S. *Eskimo,* an elderly British frigate. Inside, the tugboat *Bermuda* marks the western end of the starting line.

Tension mounts out in the starting area. For outsiders it may seem that we swarm around completely aimlessly, all of the ships. But for us it is a matter of working up to the best possible starting position.

Some of the great ships remain far in the background, among them the *Kruzenshtern* and the *Danmark*. *Kruzenshtern* appears to be making 'a flying start,' with a long running approach. She did the same thing out of Santa Cruz. Most of the vessels, among them the *Christian Radich,* are fighting for a favorable position by the windward mark – as in a small-boat regatta.

Using small sails and the engine, we move slowly toward the starting line. I have American film photographers and reporters on board, and they eagerly preserve this unique sight for posterity – all of these beautiful square-riggers, which are now maneuvering for a start that in the world of sailing ships would be remembered as 'the Battle of Bermuda.'

We have staysails and lower topsails set. The boys are ready in the topsail halyards. When first we set sails, it has to be done like clockwork. The tension increases. We sail towards the line at four to five knots. The wind abates somewhat. I have *Tovarishch* to port, and the *Eagle* is coming up on the starboard quarter. Behind the *Eagle* I see the square-rigger *Libertad* from Argentina, coming along with everything set except her royals. She presses in between us and H.M.S. *Eskimo*.

Suddenly things begin to happen. *Gazela Primeiro,* a former Portuguese fishing vessel used on the Newfoundland Banks and now belonging to the Philadelphia Maritime Museum, overtakes us to starboard. She comes in close

The Juan Sebastian's fore-staysail sustains too great a load in the collision with 'Libertad', and the whole foremast comes down. There were men in the rigging, and it was a miracle that only one man was injured.

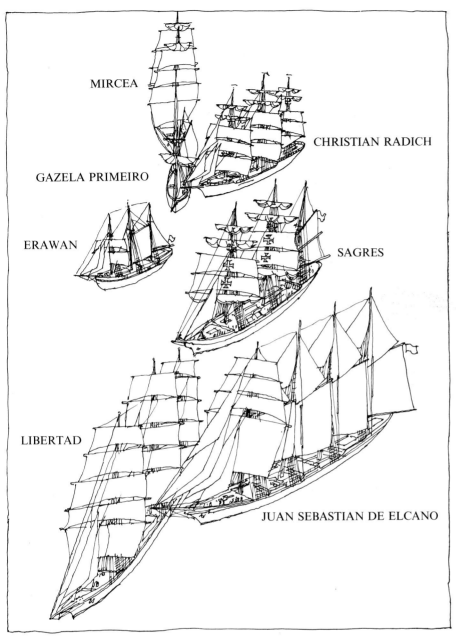

MIRCEA

CHRISTIAN RADICH

GAZELA PRIMEIRO

ERAWAN

SAGRES

LIBERTAD

JUAN SEBASTIAN DE ELCANO

Situation sketch based on the air photograph showing the two collisions. Sketch: Kai Øvre

to the side of the ship, and I ask her to get away – loudly and clearly, in my best English: 'Get out of my way!'

She obeys, turns hard starboard, and collides with *Mircea,* a large square-rigger from Rumania. The smaller *Gazela Primeiro*'s rigging is destroyed by the *Mircea*'s bowsprit. Up on our port side comes a Panama-registered ship, named *Erawan,* which reverses her engines with all sails set. She loses control of her steering and comes right under our bowsprit. To starboard *Gazela* is being pressed against our bow by *Mircea,* which also, with all sails set, rings astern on her engine and loses control over her steering.

For a moment I'm afraid that *Gazela* will be crushed between *Mircea* and us, but our powerful new engine, which screams into reverse, just manages to back us out, clear of a collision.

Up on the fo'c'sle the chief officer thinks that the *Mircea*'s bowsprit will take our fore rigging. He orders all men under the fo'c'sle. A sound man from the American TV team runs aft on the boat deck and jumps over the railing and down to the main deck, loaded with his heavy equipment. From there he sprints

The boys giving all they've got on the mizzen-topgallant halyards.   PHOTOGRAPH: FINN BERGAN

to the place he thinks must be the safest, the quarterdeck, at the captain's side. Normally he would have half-killed himself with a jump like that, but it is obvious that panic has given him enormous strength. The *Libertad* gets called back for a restart. She has crossed too early and is lying with the rest of the fleet on the port. In the midst of all this confusion the *Libertad* turns to port. This is the one thing she shouldn't do. What the hell is she thinking of! The *Libertad* cuts across our bow and disappears behind the wall of sails on our port side. Back there the *Libertad* and the *Juan Sebastian de Elcano* collide, and the *Sebastian* loses her fore-topmast, with men in the rigging.

We back out of the mess and wait until the 'battle' is over. Half an hour later the wrecks are on their way out of the area, and we cross the starting line. The remnants of the *Gazela*'s mainmast pulled our starboard topsail brace loose and made a small hole in the fore-topsail. The crew is already at work splicing in new ropes. There is a hellish cackling over the radio. Everyone is talking at once. I hear that no one has been killed in this crazy start. One cadet on the *Sebastian* was injured. This could have been a catastrophe.

In full sail with a gentle breeze.
PHOTOGRAPH: HARALD TUSBERG

The binnacle in which the compass is housed. The compass card is lit by a kerosene lamp beside the binnacle. The iron balls are quadrant correctors for the compass deviation.
PHOTOGRAPH: KAI ØVRE

VI

SECOND PLACE OVERALL

Less than a day later we are again number three, but this time after the *Gorch Fock* and the *Dar Pormorza*.

At the captains' meeting yesterday we were briefed on the weather situation by a team from the American weather forecasting service in Norfolk. We saw satellite pictures with infrared photography of the Gulf Stream. It will be necessary to utilize this warm, northbound ocean current, which makes it possible to live in our country. The meteorological prognoses promised fairly good weather conditions on the last stretch of the sailing race, the 640 nautical miles to Newport, Rhode Island. Quite a day, to be sure!

I leave the quarterdeck only when I can no longer see a square-sail on the horizon. When the darkness falls, the radar screen is watched extra carefully.

The wind stands from a southeasterly direction with a force of two to three for two days. On June 22, at 1600 hours, the logbook reads: 'Calm, clear. Temp. 30 ° centigrade, variable courses.' This means that we are drifting. The barometer is high, and there is nothing to indicate any immediate changes in the weather. The prognoses from Norfolk do not hold good. We have the most marvelous sunshine, heat, and high, blue sky. We are not complaining, but it is not what you could really call racing weather. Not at all what we were promised.

The ship has fallen into her own rhythm again. Watch follows watch, and everything is as it should be on board. The chief officer and I exercise with the boys, who have now begun to like this daily round of sweating. They like it that we join them and share their exertions. In this way we make better contact with the boys, too. I am training the rowing team that is going to show its stuff at Newport. They feel privileged. Only ten men have been chosen from the eighty-seven. Several of our American guests have now been bitten by the exercising bug, too, and take part. 'When in Rome, do as the Romans do.' We also try to work damage control exercises and lifeboat drill into the routine, at least while we are at sea. Ashore, there is no chance for this, as the visiting program is too hectic.

The next day it is again quiet, without a ripple on the blue-and-silver surface of the ocean. A formation of dolphins is playing around the ship, in mutually respectful distance from a shark, which is following the vessel. A shark following the ship! This was not a good omen in the old days: somebody on board was going to die. Just old superstition, of course, but ... I am against the unnecessary killing of living beings, but I pretend that I do not see a sharkhook being slung over the railing. The bait is slightly rotten salt pork, which has been lying across the brine in the barrel. The shark won't eat fresh meat from dinner. After having inspected the bait and taken a look at the leader of chain, he opens his jaw over the hook and strikes. The hook is in the corner of his jaw. I can't stand it any longer. I take the line myself and pull the seven-foot fish to midship, where the gangway davit is rigged up. Halfway, his grip loosens. The hook, minus bait, is the only thing left on the line. The shark is evidently injured. He dives straight down into the depths. The pilot fish that has kept alongside the shark the whole time can't manage to keep up. A solitary barracuda, which has also been following along in the shadow of the ship, is now absolute ruler.

We are now in the same situation as we were at the end of the race to Bermuda. The wind has disappeared, and it is clear that we will not now reach Newport by the time set. Again there is a discussion with the race committee, but this time they are more obliging. Following a poll among the captains by radio, the race is called off for the Class-A ships at 1900 hours, on June 24. Our position is then 36 ° 27 ′N by 66 ° 37 ′W.

We start up our main engine and chug towards Newport. Our feelings of anticipation about what is going to happen in the United States during the next few weeks begin to build up. I take out the program for the hundredth time. Is there anything we have forgotten or have overlooked?

The next day, Friday, June 25, at 1405 hours, we shut down our main engine.

The stock anchor is catted, with the cat tackle behind. PHOTOGRAPH: KAI ØVRE

We now have wind; a good reach gives us eight to nine knots. I stay in contact with the two vessels ahead of us, the *Gorch Fock* and the *Dar Pormorza*.

Our radar cuts out, and this means that the fog is creeping in and the wind is falling off. There is fog all night. What is worst is the knowledge that the Newport–Bermuda race is in progress. Hundreds of boats are on their way to Bermuda on the course opposite to ours. These small boats don't usually have radar. We keep a steady lookout, as well as we can in that fog.

I'm glad the race was called off. The finish line is located way in by shore, and navigating in these waters without radar but with strong ocean currents is something I can well do without.

The following noon we approach land. A small breeze blows up, and the fog disappears. In brilliant weather we see the coast of North America off Newport rise up from the sun-quivering horizon. We set all sails and sail towards land while thousands of pleasure craft come out to welcome us. 'Welcome to America.' 'Thank you for coming; beautiful ship you have.'

By radio and from megaphones we are welcomed. Whistles and electric horns toot and blare. Channel 16 (the emergency channel for the radiotelephone) is hideous – zero radio discipline! This resembles the furor we heard following the 'battle of Bermuda.'

Newport has called all her pilots in, but with the large fleet, which wants to enter the harbor more or less all at the same time, we have to wait awhile. I respectfully wave old Jurkiewich on the *Dar Pormorza* in front of me. He was so kind as to 'talk me in' on radar in the fog yesterday. Besides, he is senior captain and, as such, commands respect.

Top: An armada of pleasure craft from Newport welcomed the ship to America – as they did wherever the boys sailed.

PHOTOGRAPHS: WILLIAM RHYINS

Evening mood with large and small ships at anchor at Newport.

At 1622 hours (4:22 P.M.) on Saturday, June 26, the pilot comes aboard. Again: 'Welcome to America, Captain.' 'Thank you, Pilot.'

With furled sails we glide into the harbor, using our engine. The port is teeming. That everything goes all right is due, to a large extent, to sheer luck. Thousands of small boats dash in all directions. In the air, planes, helicopters, airships, and autogiros are flying around. I don't know what sort of steering rules they have agreed upon, up there, but to a simple seaman there appears to be complete confusion.

A beautiful schooner with the lovely name of *Shenandoah* sails up alongside starboard for full sail. She has something of the *Bluenose* lines to her – ships that were constructed along the line of the old fishing schooners from the Grand Banks – efficient, requiring small crews to handle the rigging, and built-in speed. The first ship to reach port gets the best price for her catch. The man at the wheel of *Shenandoah* doffs his cap in respect for his ship's square-rigged big sister, as he passes. He also dips his flag – the flag of the country of which we are now the guests.

We have to go all the way into the narrow harbor, turn, and go alongside the *Eagle,* the hostship for the square-riggers. Two tugs help us to turn around. Tens of thousands of people along the piers and beaches watch the fleet coming in from the sea, the fleet that will honor America on her special, festive day.

'Finished at the helm, finished with engines.' We are in America.

Newport is an old seaport – at least, she is old by American standards. The city authorities are expecting large crowds of tourists and visitors who want to see the Tall Ships. They expect traffic chaos, and their expectations are fulfilled. It is almost impossible to get anywhere by car – you have to walk.

Margrethe and I are to marry in a few days, in New York. She has come over from Norway and is here in Newport. But we have to go to New York in order to take blood tests and arrange the marriage license, and so we slip off one day. Drive, at a snail's pace, to a small airfield outside the city. Take a taxi plane to the main airport, where we get seats on a plane to Kennedy Airport. The Norwegian Merchant Fleet chaplain in New York, Leiv Gundersen, whom I already know and who is going to marry us, has made all the necessary arrangements. We meet him at the Seamen's Church in Brooklyn.

At Newport the Sail Training Association has finished its work. The race is over, and I am given the third prize for the final leg and second prize overall. The *Tovarishch* was fifth this time but is best overall. The awards are given at Fort John, outside the city. I have suggested to STA that, on this occasion, we should honor that grand old man, Captain Jurkiewich of the *Dar Pormorza.* He will sail his last trip when he later returns home across the Atlantic. I had previously been given a nice painting of the *Dar Pormorza* as a gift by one of the STA members. I have asked him if he would mind my giving this painting to Jurkiewich. No, he said, he liked the idea. At the awards presentation I ask to speak, as the youngest captain of the Tall Ships, and give Jurkiewich the painting of his ship. On the port side of the *Dar Pormorza* are seen the White Cliffs of Dover, as the ship sails north up the Channel. The picture is called *Sailing Home.* Jurkiewich is very moved when he comes up to receive the picture.

The youngsters participate in rowing, tugs-of-war, swimming, and a lot of other activities. One day they go to Mystic Seaport, which has gradually been built into a large maritime museum. It was from here that Erling Brunborg took the old rescue ship *Sandefjord* a few years ago and sailed her to Norway.

The captains are called in for a final STA meeting. We express our thanks and say goodbye to the Englishmen who have carried on their great work with this year's Atlantic race. They are to watch the parade in New York before returning to their country by air.

The capstan, or spindle, is used when the anchor is weighed. Bars are inserted in the holes at the top of the capstan, and the anchor is weighed using hand and foot power.

PHOTOGRAPH: KAI ØVRE

Liberty. It doesn't take long to make contact with 'the natives,' particularly the girls. Language barriers just don't exist.
PHOTOGRAPH: STIG NÆSS

PHOTOGRAPH: WILLIAM RHYINS

The last Operation Sail with international participation was held in New York in 1964. The *Christian Radich* was there, with Captain Kjeld Backen as skipper. The key men on the planning staff from 1964 have been behind Operation Sail 1976. In 1964 there was a small group of enthusiasts who did all the work with no remuneration – volunteers, who thought that it was worth all the effort to see the square-riggers parade in New York harbor. It was a success then, and it was later proposed to repeat this during the anniversary in 1976 – the 200th anniversary.

OPSAIL-76, which is the contraction of the organization's name, is, or was, a completely private organization, whose objective was to get as many as possible of the world's sailing ships to take part in a parade in New York Harbor on July 4, 1976.

Gradually, interest in this idea grew. The few key men who started the whole thing needed more people. The U.S. Navy was to celebrate the day with an international naval revue, also in New York Harbor. Naval vessels from the whole world were invited to send representatives. Norway was to send K.N.M.

Trondheim. All of this was coordinated, and both the U.S. Navy and the U.S. Coast Guard were brought into the planning. The whole affair began to take on enormous proportions. New York's authorities began to perceive the contours of a gigantic arrangement, for which millions of people would pour into the port districts. What does one do with traffic control, security, police surveillance, and other supervisory measures that are necessary to remain in control of it all? What if terrorists were to start some sort of devilment on a day like that? It was a thought that made cold shivers run up and down their spines.

OPSAIL-76 has a briefing for the captains before we set sail. We go through the program in detail. We are to make a turn into the harbor area in Newport, in a semicircle, to show the thousands of onlookers the fleet, before we sail westward along the beaches of Long Island, where more thousands – even hundreds of thousands – have gathered on the shore to see a fleet of sailing ships, the likes of which they know they will never see again. We are asked to sail 'in company, close to the shores.'

The last day in Newport, June 30, we give a large reception on board. Our guests of honor are Crown Prince Harald and Crown Princess Sonja, accompanied by, among others, our ambassador to Washington, S. Chr. Sommerfelt.

That evening there is the 'ball of the year' in Newport. All of the captains are invited. Twelve hundred guests are to be entertained at the stately home Rosecliff, a house with an aura of old wealth, which is still kept in first-class condition. No establishment can feed all the guests at one time, so we are spread around restaurants all over the city. Margrethe and I are to eat at the Black Pearl. I borrow a limousine from the information service. We do not know where the Black Pearl is. We have to walk in all our finery to the car, which cannot push through the crowds to the pier. Then we drive two blocks, and there is the Black Pearl.

Getting from the restaurant to Rosecliff is a bigger problem. No car, and it is several kilometers to the house. We end up in a small truck, which belongs to a boatyard nearby. We arrive, with three other couples, sitting on bags of sails. The driver sweeps up to the main entrance, where the servants, without moving a facial muscle, open the back door and see eight gala-clad people crawl across sail bags and try to descend elegantly from the truck.

I meet Nick at the ball. He does not look as though he feels completely at home in his newly purchased uniform. He appears in an American naval uniform with a captain's insignia. He has bought all his finery at a very reasonable price at a military depot.

He tells us about the period when he was becalmed before reaching Bermuda. He had stopped two ships before he was given fuel enough to continue by engine to Bermuda. 'But what about food – and water?' 'Oh, we managed,' he says. Besides, he had a case of whiskey as emergency rations. I tell Nick that I am going to get married in New York. He looks at me compassionately and implies that sunstroke has a lot of funny results.

Proud boys with the second prize.
PHOTOGRAPH: ØIVIND BARBO

Opposite page: Tied up at South Street Seaport Museum are, left to right, the 'Libertad', the 'Esmeralda', front center the 'Gloria', and behind her the 'Christian Radich'.
PHOTOGRAPH: SHOSTAL ASSOCIATES

VII

MAGNIFICENT DAYS IN NEW YORK

The next morning we are to set sail. The fog is as thick as the traditional pea soup, and we have to delay our departure. Not until afternoon does it lift enough that we can get out. Unfortunately, we have to disappoint the many people on Long Island. The visibility is very poor, and we chug toward Ambrose Lighthouse at the entrance to New York Harbor. On July 3 we are piloted in to our allotted anchorage at Sandy Hook, this natural breakwater of sand that has been washed up to form a safe harbor.

We greet the *Nippon Maru*. She is a four-masted bark and has sailed for four months from her homeland of Japan to be a guest in America.

The whole day is spent washing, polishing, scrubbing, and oiling all over the whole fleet. In the evening the local yacht clubs invite everyone to parties in their clubhouses. We make pretty speeches to each other and wish each other good luck on the morrow.

Sunday, July 4, 1976. The weather is clear, and I get up early. What is happening in that big city over there in the shimmering sun? What will meet us when we come into port?

Two large speedboats come alongside. They have guests on board who are to accompany us during the parade. Margrethe is among them. They turned out at 0400 hours in order to steer clear of the traffic chaos later on.

Pilots are put aboard the ships. New York pilots have called in all their reserves and have eighty men at their disposal, who have been shuttling back and forth since the naval vessels came in yesterday morning. It is a bit of a coincidence that our pilot was on board the *Christian Radich* in 1964 also.

We weigh anchor according to the program. U.S.C.G.S. *Eagle* is to lead the parade, followed by the *Danmark,* the *Christian Radich,* and all the others.

The Class-A ships are to sail in one line, the Class-B in two lines, and the Class-C in four. In all, there will be approximately three hundred ships and boats. The naval vessels taking part in the international naval revue are anchored along the route from Verazano Bridge to the George Washington Bridge up the Hudson River. The distance is nineteen nautical miles, and the parade will take five hours.

A few cables inside Verazano Bridge is the U.S.S. *Forrestal,* a modern aircraft carrier of 80,000 tons. On board is the American president, Gerald Ford, plus 3,000 VIPs from all over the world. Our crown prince and princess are among these very important people. The crown princess's birthday is today. We have sent flowers, which we hope arrive in time.

At 1100 hours on the dot, the *Eagle* sails under Verazano Bridge, and the show is on. We have unfurled all sails, but unfortunately the wind direction is too sharp for square sails. The staysails will have to do, and they have been lashed in so the wind barely catches. We are to keep 600 yards' distance from the *Danmark* ahead of us. There is a lot of manipulating with the control handle to keep a decent station, without too great and sudden changes in speed, which would spoil things for the ship coming astern. For a moment I remember my training in formation sailing with destroyers, in my midshipman days, twenty-five years in the past. If anyone had told me at that time that I would be trying something similar, but on board a square-rigger, twenty-five years from then, and in New York Harbor, I would have said he was completely crazy.

We are to 'man the railings' in passing the U.S.S. *Forrestal.* The youngsters are to be placed at spaced intervals, from way out on the bowsprit, along the railing to the quarterdeck, where the officers are lined up. I see that most of the other vessels are manning the yards, but we don't have the supporting wires that the boys can hold onto, standing on the yards. I have one cadet who plays the trumpet. He has brought his instrument on board, and I use him to blow 'Attention' on formal occasions. The last time was during the visit of the crown prince and crown princess in Newport. The boy is named Erik Blom, and he comes from the old naval city of Horten. Fifteen minutes before we pass the

The bowsprit, or the jibboom, with the safety net stretched. Beneath the figurehead is the bob stay, and under this the jib stay, which reaches all the way out to the jibboom yardarm.

PHOTOGRAPH: KAI ØVRE

A formally clothed Lady with all of her 'skirts' set and the Stars and Stripes on the mainmast, ready to parade.

Forrestal I have an idea. All of the ships are giving the correct honors. We are to do that, also, but maybe we can add a little extra to the day by doing something original, even though it may not be so militarily correct? A plane has written 'happy birthday' in the sky, with sky-writing. 'Happy birthday' – hey, that's the idea! Get hold of Erik! He appears immediately. 'Can you play Happy Birthday?'

'Nah – yeah, maybe. Can I have ten minutes to try?'

'OK, but not one second more.'

He dashes away and comes up after a couple of minutes.

'I *think* maybe I can do it.'

He *thinks* he can, I say to myself, and if he can't it will sound awfully silly.

We approach the *Forrestal*. The boys are ordered into position. Erik is ordered aloft on the main-royal. From there he first blows the correct 'Attention,' and after that Happy Birthday, so that it echoes all over the harbor. Happy birthday to America – and to our countrywoman, who, we hope, has received our flowers.

All around us the small Coast Guard boats are swarming like watchdogs – to supervise the approximately 30,000 pleasure craft of all sizes and shapes that are out to greet the fleet. I am impressed at the discipline and seamanship these pleasure-boat skippers show. Most of them have realized that it is best to drop anchor. And along with the anchored naval vessels, they form an avenue down which we sail. All commercial traffic has been stopped for today and tomorrow in New York Harbor. This was necessary in order to hold the parade, have enough berth space for the guests, and have full traffic control in the harbor. An impressive plan. People have been told on TV and on the radio in the last few days just how the parade and the arrangements in conjunction with this are to be held. They have been well informed, and the whole affair goes along smoothly.

At 1400 hours the salute is heard from all naval vessels entitled to salute – twenty-one shots, as an ovation to this great country on her 200th birthday. It is remarkably quiet while the salute is given, aside from the sound of the guns themselves. We can feel the solemnity of the occasion. Something bigger than just this parade of ships from all over the world – reflections about and gratitude to their forefathers, who created this country.

Even the 'Christian Radich' looks small against New York's skyline.

Along the shores of the whole harbor area there are 7 million people watching the parade, a sight never to be forgotten, and I believe that, just then, the Americans feel a solidarity and pride in what they and their forefathers have made of this continent – in spite of schism and dispiritedness at political scandals such as Watergate, the unhappy Vietnam war, etc.

We dip our flag in respect for the New World that has accepted so many Norwegian immigrants.

The K.N.M. *Trondheim* is lying near the Statue of Liberty. My friend Captain Kaare Julian Granmar is captain on board. We sailed together in the hard old days. His crew mans the railings for us. Definitely not regulation, but we like it.

Behind the Statue of Liberty we can see Ellis Island, the island where immigrants were registered and checked before they were allowed to enter God's

On the way up the Hudson River, the 'Danmark' ahead.

There's no doubt we are in Manhattan, with airships and sky-high buildings . . .

Own Country. Many a poor Norwegian has landed here, with his bundles and his family. They were not met by the welcome that meets us! Those who came over with the first immigrant vessel, the *Restauration,* were arrested for having too many people aboard. Many of the descendants of those immigrants who went through Ellis Island are lining the shores today and welcoming the fleet.

We pass Battery Park, where the viewers have paid twenty-five dollars a ticket. A flowerbed of spectators. The Norwegian colony has drummed up a number of people who are waving Norwegian flags down below the One World Trade Center on Lower Manhattan.

Astern, we can see a forest of masts and sails on the huge fleet, which is gradually moving up the Hudson River. A cruiser passes close to on her way

Most of the ships 'man the yards' in the parade.

The tugs are superfluous as we turn the ship ourselves in the Hudson River.
PHOTOGRAPH: STIG NÆSS

The Statue of Liberty, symbol of hope and optimism, which meets the seafarer in New York Harbor. Many an emigrant has seen this statue at the portal of a new world.

Expectant formation before the 'Christian Radich' ties up in southern Manhattan at the South Street Seaport Museum.

down. We greet each other politely, two ships belonging to two different worlds and times, with the sea as our common element.

We have head winds up the Hudson River. On the trip down we intend to set all our canvas. The *Eagle* and the *Danmark* do the same. Just above the George Washington Bridge a number of tugs are ready to give the vessels a hand in turning in the narrow river. *Eagle* waves the tugboats away, turns alone. *Danmark* does the same, and so we do, too. When the wind has caught the foresails, we bring her around. She lists a little in the turn. The wind has risen a bit. The pilot has never been under sail before, so he looks extremely skeptically at our maneuvering. We come around, set all except the lower sails. I have to have complete visibility ahead, so no lower sails.

And so we pass the rest of the fleet on an opposite course. Oleg Vandenko on *Tovarishch* greets us with his flag, and we return the greeting. Schneider on *Kruzenshtern* waves his hat as we pass. Jurkiewich on *Dar Pormorza,* Van Stakkelberg on *Gorch Fock,* they all wave, and we wave back as we pass close to in this gigantic parade of ships and sails.

We pass the Class-B and Class-C boats. I wave to my friend Nick on *Artemis*. *Sir Winston Churchill* has a female crew, girls eighteen to twenty years old, who, in Captain Collis' opinion, are every bit as good seamen as the boys are. I have heard my cadets express a desire to meet the crew of the *Sir Winston Churchill*.

At the end of the parade of vessels there are different 'character boats.' We see a Viking ship, a genuine Chinese junk with an equally genuine Chinese crew. We see the copy of *Bluenose,* the famous Canadian fishing schooner. We see *Club Mediterraine,* the 230-foot one-man ship, which can make twenty-eight knots. Alain Colan, the Frenchman who sails the boat, has guests on board today, we see. Four-masted, with staysails. Operated by one man. OK, at any rate he has a lot of space on board.

It is time to lower and furl sails in order to turn to port past Governors Island, into the East River. Just inside the mouth, at the foot of Fulton Street, is our berth, at the South Street Seaport Museum. We lay there last year, during the emigrant anniversary, and I have asked if we could have the same pier space this year. Here we feel at home among the sailing ships, the chantey singers, and everything that creates a 'breath of days gone by.' With the *Eagle* and the *Danmark,* we put in alongside the pier, at 1600 hours exactly, right on schedule.

The by-now-familiar crowds of tens of thousands of spectators welcome us. This is American warmheartedness and friendliness at its best.

In the evening my mother and Margrethe's parents and brother come aboard. They have watched the parade from a yacht in the harbor. From the quarterdeck we watch the huge fireworks display, the biggest in the world, which is sent up from five different spots in the port area. Thirty-two tons of rockets go up in one half-hour – a fantastic play of color against a dark sky. A number of cameras are undoubtedly at work to immortalize this crescendo of colors that marks the finish of the Tall Ships Parade on July 4, 1976.

Three busy days remain. The boys are programmed to see more of New York

Formation for liberty inspection; the duty mate checks the cadets' uniforms. In the background, the large city that is just waiting to be investigated.

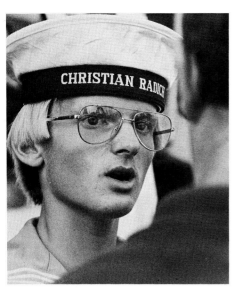

PHOTOGRAPH: WILLIAM RHYINS

in a shorter space of time than any package tourist ever gets to see. They are shown around the U.N. Building and meet Ambassador Ole Aalgaard. They attend a boxing match at Madison Square Garden. They are entertained in the American way, given culinary refinements such as hamburgers and banana splits, food that is very popular among the younger generation.

On July 5, I go to the consulate for money. Wages for the crew, lunch at the One World Trade Center, this huge building with an extremely elegant club on its top floor. Official duties fill the whole day, as usual. One must learn to live by the clock.

Besides this, we have a few small preparations for the wedding. We are going to get married on board. We do not have time to get married at the Seamen's Church in Brooklyn – don't dare take a chance on the snarled traffic we would have to go through to get there. We will have to do it on board, with the masts as the church spires.

The next day the boys are parading on Broadway, fifty of them, along with the same number from K.N.M. *Trondheim*. Young people from all of the ships and boats in the harbor form a colorful parade down this famous street, while the confetti drops down from the high skyscrapers.

The Israeli contingent from a destroyer looks very warlike, with their sidearms. I assume that they have suitably celebrated the very successful Entebbe operation carried out two days prior to this.

Following the parade to city hall, the city's mayor welcomes the marchers.

I slip away, because I am going to be married in two hours' time.

We are married on the quarterdeck. The ship's bell is used as a church bell. On the pier, several hundred people are standing, watching the ceremony. After the champagne and dinner, the vessel fills with guests, old and new friends. The greeting of flowers from the crown prince and crown princess warms our hearts.

We are aboard early the next day. We spent the night at the Waldorf Astoria Hotel, where the prices were actually the most impressive feature. Margrethe signs on, along with several of the crew members' wives, who have come to New York and are to be aboard for a couple of weeks. We were to have sailed this evening, but hear that it is difficult to get a tug before tomorrow. Actually we have only just enough time to cover the distance to the next harbor, Boston, but by figuring carefully, we find out that, with a few hundred extra revolutions of the propeller, we can get there in time. OK, we'll sail tomorrow with the *Danmark*.

All of the captains on the bigger ships are invited to the exclusive Circumnavigators Club, an organization of round-the-world sailors, round-the-world drivers, flyers, walkers, and astronauts. Whoever has crossed the meridians all around the globe can become a member. We are driven to Governors Island, where the famous round-the-world sailor Irving Johnson shows a film from a hurricane at Cape Horn, taken aboard the *Peking*.

A lot of fine adventurer types are to be found here. It is a pleasure to hear these men's stories from distant places around the globe. You really get all fired up with a desire for adventure when you're with people like these.

At lunchtime on July 8 we slip our lines, are pulled out into the river by tugs, are turned around on course, and go out the East River, sounding our ship's whistle in farewell. Full of people on the piers, waving 'au revoir' to us. Tough, hard-boiled New York has really shown us her warm nature during these last few days. There has been great hospitality, and we have made many new friends. Out in the harbor we have arranged a meeting with *Sagafjord*. We are to be 'immortalized' together, the old and the new, probably for use in advertising for the cruise trade.

We have favorable winds, set all sails, and sail side by side with the huge passenger ship at six knots. After the picture-taking is finished, our companion disappears into the haze on her way out of the harbor.

Farther out we meet the R.Y. *Britannia,* the British royal yacht. She is on her way to New York, it looks like. She is escorted by a large Coast Guard cutter that looks almost like a frigate. Out at Ambrose Lighthouse we say farewell to the *Danmark,* which is sailing south along the East Coast. We sail eastward, toward Boston.

PHOTOGRAPHS: WILLIAM RHYINS

The schooner 'Sir Winston Churchill' is the only school ship with female cadets. Here they are in a tug-of-war, strongly encouraged by the crew of the ketch 'Great Britain'.
PHOTOGRAFPH LEO DE WYS

Thirty-two tons of fireworks shot up in the course of half an hour.

PHOTOGRAPH FROM: TALL SHIPS

And then they were married . . .

It is July 10, ten o'clock in the morning. We managed to just make the beginning of a miniparade of sailing ships into Boston Harbor. Queen Elizabeth is present as five square-riggers, led by the U.S.S. *Constellation,* enter the harbor under full sail. We are alloted pier space at Army Pier, a fenced-in harbor area used for shipping supplies to the U.S. Army, wherever it might be around the world.

The two days the ship is to lie in Boston we have 'open ship.' People begin to take their places in line at 9:00 A.M. The gates are not open until 1:00 P.M. The police report that 200,000 are standing in line by that time. It looks as though the ethnic groups in the city have distributed themselves among their homeland's ships, naturally enough. We are visited by thousands with Norwegian forebears, and I can see that the *Dar Pormorza* is being invaded by Polish descendants from the city and the district. The local Sons of Norway organization takes care of the youngsters. They have a fine day outdoors, with a grill party and young hostesses. Some of the cadets are invited to a party on board the *Sir Winston Churchill.* They are entertained by the female crew. But I have a faint suspicion that our sixteen-year-olds are considered slightly too young by the English girls. Three or four years' difference in age 'the wrong way,' at that age, is a lot.

The huge stream of visitors to the ships has created traffic chaos far outside the harbor area. We have ordered bunkers from a tank truck, which requires ten hours to force its way through the crowd. A police escort is of no use. Traffic has simply stopped moving.

We finally bunker in the morning of July 12, and our departure is set for 1800 hours (6:00 P.M.). A tug is to help us turn in the narrow harbor. There is a fair wind out to sea, and, while we turn, we begin to set sail. The boys know that large numbers of film cameras are aimed at us. Television cameras are in place at the end of the pier. They work as best they can, these boys, and we pass by the other ships, waving farewell to them under full sail. Now we are on our way alone, on our trip to the Great Lakes.

Celebrations of the bicentennial are going on all over America, of course. About forty cities have asked for visits by the Tall Ships after the parade in New York. Most of the vessels are visiting the cities along the East Coast. Only the *Christian Radich* has planned a tour on the Great Lakes.

The planning has been going on for a long time, and the whole matter was finally determined when the Norwegian State promised financial aid. The director of Østlandets Skoleskib, Kjeld Backen, who was the captain on the trip to the U.S.A. in 1964, had also been on the Lakes. Now it was my privilege to take the ship to eight ports in there, in the middle of North America.

That is all we have time for. After that stormy trip home last year, I want to fix September 1 as the date of departure from the U.S. However, we extend the tour to September 8, which gives us six weeks on fresh water.

From Boston our route goes directly to Montreal, Canada. We get a real pea-souper of a fog off Nova Scotia. In order to save time we take the Canso Canal and come out in brilliant sunshine into Saint Lawrence Bay. It is about 1,400 miles from Boston to Montreal, and we are delayed seven hours in our sailing plan. The strong current in the Saint Lawrence River has fooled us.

The pilots from Les Escoumains are French-Canadians, and we already can notice the sharp feelings of opposition existing between them and the English-speaking section of the population in Canada.

At Trois Rivières, the mouth of the Saint Lawrence River, we trade pilots for the last time before Montreal. Part of our delay is due to the fact that we have had to anchor in the river in a current running six knots, just a few cables from the pier.

The chief engineer reports that the water-cooler intake is blocked up. The engine is in danger of overheating. I inform the pilot. 'We have to anchor, Pilot.' He looks at me. 'Not here, Captain.' 'Yes, right here.' He calls the traffic control

The bridal couple.

in the harbor and is given permission. He doesn't like it, but neither do I. The filter in the seawater intake is cleaned, and we can weigh anchor. Fortunately our weak windlass manages the job. I promise the pilot a drink when we put into the dock. 'Please, sir, not one – two!'

There is a strike among the tugboat crews in Montreal, so we have to manage by ourselves. My good friend and best man, Bjørn Kvisgaard, and his beautiful wife, Bente, are in the group to welcome us on the pier, to our delight. Bjørn is the enthusiastic leader of the export council of Norway's New York office. Last year he was responsible for a number of arrangements on board the ship, under the auspices of the export council, and on the Lakes he is to be in charge of similar arrangements at some of the ports.

It is Olympics time in Montreal. The Seamen's Church arranges a meeting between our youngsters and the Norwegian Olympic teams. General Bangstad, who is the head of the troupe, makes a speech, and we from the *Radich* wish the sportsmen good luck in the coming competitions. The youngsters are given tickets to the next day's soccer game between Brazil and Spain. This is supposed to be a really good game, say people who know something about it. At any rate, they will get to see a little of the gigantic installation, which has cost millions of dollars more than had been estimated. Surely, the limits must be reached pretty soon as to how much a country can spend on arrangements like this.

In Montreal we make the ship ready for the trip on the Great Lakes. We take chemical toilets aboard, according to seaway regulations. The two stern lifeboats, which hang off the ship's side, are taken ashore. In the locks they can be crushed against the walls. Otherwise, there are the usual supplementary supplies of provisions, water, fuel. We will be using our engine for the most part, in the days to come, although we will sail at every opportunity.

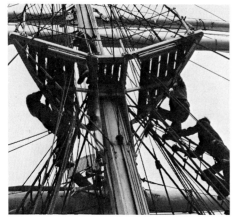

The foremast's top is entered. Ratlines on the shrouds for hands and feet. Futtock shrouds run from the mast and out on the top and must be entered at an angle outwards.
PHOTOGRAPH: KAI ØVRE

The foremast and the mainmast, or more correctly, the topgallant masts on the foremast and the mainmast, are lowered about fifteen feet. This is to enable us to get under the bridges in the Saint Lawrence Seaway. Formerly, they used to take down the two upper yards, the topgallant and the royal, before the mast was lowered. We make a try at loosening the rigging screws that hold the mast, lift this an inch, take away the stop-bolt, and lower the whole thing with the yards still intact. This works very well and saves us a lot of unnecessary work. This operation will have to be repeated five times later on. We say goodbye for the time being to Montreal. We are coming back here again, on our way out. We turn into the canal system and the first lock. Based on the experiences of the last trip the *Radich* had on the lakes, we have a tugboat as a fender against the lock wall. We have a small one of forty-five feet. This must be a strikebreaker, because all of the tugs in Montreal are lying at the buoys. This boat proves to be of little or no use, so I let him return. It does not look as though the two men on board there mind at all, after they have almost tipped over between us and the lock wall. After this we use mooring ropes to the lock walls on both sides. We see to it that the ship stays in the center while the lock is flooding, and this works fine.

The next day we sail through the Thousand Islands district. A vacationer's paradise for relatively wealthy people from the large cities around the lakes. Idyllic, small islands with luxuriant vegetation and summer homes all over them – houses of all types, including chateaulike buildings inspired by Europe's fortresses from the Middle Ages. A formidable fleet of pleasure boats accompanies us. The local radio station broadcasts position reports on the *Radich* at regular intervals, and while in the locks, particularly, we have a great many spectators. There is no doubt that we often feel that we are on exhibition. It is an odd feeling to sail on these man-made canals. The canal system winds through typical farming country on certain stretches. The smell of grass and hay is in the air. We can hear the cattle lowing from the herds in the pastures. Many Norwegians have sailed here for the Norwegian shipping companies, which, until a few years ago, had a lot of traffic on the lakes. The pilots say that there has been a general drop in traffic for several years now. The trailers have stolen much of the goods transport, but in the last two years the ore traffic and the shipments of grain have begun to increase. The newest lakers are 60,000 tonners, and they are very noticeable in the landscape, to say the least. When they are in the locks, there is a five-foot clearance on either side and just a few feet fore and aft. The sides of the ships are completely smooth, so that nothing can catch on them from the uneven lock walls. The traffic runs at full speed eight months of the year. During the four winter months that the lakes and the lock systems are frozen, the pilots and ships' crews are free. They earn fairly good wages, and several of the pilots I talked with have summer homes in Florida, which they use in the wintertime.

We sail past Kingston, where the regatta lanes for the Olympic races are. We have been invited to anchor in the harbor to act as 'decoration' during the games, but we do not have time for that. The *Radich* sails out onto Lake Ontario, the first of the five Great Lakes. We have planned to use the Welland Canal during the day, when a lot of people will be able to see the ship on her way up the locks to Lake Erie.

The skylight lets in light and air to the galley.
PHOTOGRAPH: KAI ØVRE

On Saturday, July 24, early in the morning, we approach Port Welland. We cut down speed as we approach the entrance. The controllable-pitch propeller refuses to work. We cannot reduce the pitch angle on the blades.

The chief engineer inspects it, and finally he finds out that the chain gear on the hydraulic pump, which produces the pressure enabling us to change direction, has given way. There is only one thing to do – drop anchor. The pilot lets her drift slowly into her anchorage near the canal system. We are lying a couple of miles west of the entrance, and what do we do now? The pilot says that, at the other end of the Welland Canal, up near Port Colborne in Lake Erie, there is a yard that may possibly be able to help. But it is the weekend, and they don't work on Saturdays, even here in America. The pilot sees the worn chain, and suddenly he remembers that a hardware store owner he knows in Port Welland may possibly have something like this. He goes ashore with the chief. Fortunately, we get hold of both the chain and people to install the system.

At 2200 hours we can continue into the Welland Canal, in the dark, to the great disappointment of all of the thousands of people who have been waiting the whole day.

Commander Desmond de Castro of Buffalo, whom we are to visit on our way out in about a month, appears with a bumboat up in the locks. He thinks that we will need it in the toughest of the locks, where it won't be possible to throttle the flooding valves – in the so-called Flight Locks. We use the bumboat as a fender, but we really don't get much use out of it. Our crew is trained to keep the ship in the middle of the lock, so we are self-reliant. The bumboat stays with us until Port Colborne, however. Then we say goodbye and *au revoir* to Commander de Castro. We raise the topgallant masts underway, thereby making up for the time we lost just before the Welland Canal.

For several days we have not been able to send our garbage ashore. They are very strict about pollution on the lakes, which is understandable. It was really at the last possible moment that they became aware of the strong pollution industry creates by letting its waste go into the lakes. In Lake Ontario we have seen dead fish floating around with bloated bellies. I contact the port authorities in Detroit, to learn if it would be possible to get a boat to come and fetch our plastic bags full of garbage. The end of the story is that the police take on the job. Two policeboats put out, and they are friendliness incarnate, even in their role as garbage collectors.

Probably not regulation laundering of T-shirts, but they get clean with strong soap and a brush.
<small>PHOTOGRAPH: FINN BERGAN</small>

Opposite page: Washing clothes with the whole of Lake Michigan at our disposal, in Sutton Bay, where the ship is being dressed up for her introduction to Chicago.

Our white ship runs on her engine up the Detroit River, over across Lake Saint Clair, under the bridge in Port Huron, where the current runs strong. Here we meet Lake Huron, whose name reminds me of my boyhood Indian stories. We have a fair wind out on the lake, and we set our sails, to the joy of the pilot. His only chance to sail with a square-rigger in these waters. We are followed by radio. The reports are sent out at regular intervals, and, when, in the evening, we steer our way for full sail through the Mackinac Strait, we are met by the usual fleet of pleasure craft. West of Mackinac Strait we meet Lake Michigan. In the north is the state of Wisconsin, where a great many Scandinavians have settled. We are in the middle of the ancient Indian country. Here is where the white man introduced the scalping of 'Redskins.' The Indians thought this was a good custom and decorated their belts with the scalps of white men. Nature is very fertile here. The big forests stand all the way down to the shore wherever people have not made roads or plowed the land. White birch trunks gleam through all of the greenery.

The wind drops. We lower and furl our sails, start up the engine, and wind our way between the buoys that mark the shallows here at the north end of the lake. The sun sinks behind the forest-clad hills over there in the west, and while the night air carries the scent of forest and field our bow plows its way across Lake Michigan.

We have a lot of spare time before our call at the next port, Chicago. I have really studied the chart to find a quiet anchorage where we can anchor and do a little bit of ship's work. The vessel needs paint along her sides after the lock trips, the teak needs a coating of oil, the hammocks need to be washed, and a general washing of clothes for the youngsters is necessary.

Our anchor drops in Sutton Bay at four o'clock in the morning. On the map it looks as though there are very few inhabitants in the vicinity, which is just what we want. We are wrong. There is a small town, just inland, very poorly marked on the map. A vacation spot, maybe, because the boats swarm out to us. The owners say that they couldn't believe their eyes when they awoke to the sight of a square-rigger, anchored out in the bay.

The district around here is known for its sweet cherries and sour cherries. It is cherrytime, and the local grocer comes out with a case as a gift to the ship. He tosses it over to one of the youngsters, who is washing the side of the ship from a lifeboat. He misses, and the cherries disappear into the deep. No dirty looks because of this, however. The grocer goes ashore for a new case, which is brought on board.

The journalistic nose cannot be denied. Our completely unofficial working visit is a welcome piece of news for the local paper. Reporter and photographer come chugging out before we have eaten breakfast.

We have a fine day, during which a lot of good work is done. The weather gods are in a good mood, as usual, and we waste a lot of fresh water. But we have all of Lake Michigan at our disposal.

A good, sun-warmed breeze is blowing. Clothes, woolen blankets, and hammocks are hanging to dry in the rigging and over the railing. We have complete confidence in Him who directs the weather. If there is rain now, there is little possibility of drying. The workday ends with swabbing down the decks with soap. They dry quickly, and the teak is light and gleaming.

Before the evening meal we let the whole flock of boys take a bath. There is a lifeboat ready, with a lookout who keeps an eye on the bathers. Whether or not he really can manage this in the welter of arms and legs that jump over the railing and splash around like playful puppies is another matter. Our wives also take a swim with the boys.

After supper the whole ship quiets down. She gleams in the evening sun, looks at her reflection in the bay, is satisfied with her appearance; she is ready to be introduced to the big city of Chicago.

Early in the morning on July 31, we weigh anchor and sail out from Sutton Bay. A couple of solitary fishermen are out to wave farewell to us. We have lots of time and prefer to sail, since the wind is favorable later in the morning. The weather can be very variable here on the lakes. We have heard about sudden thunderstorms, with heavy rains. We get one like this. The chief officer is on watch. The wind suddenly drops and switches direction. The sails slam back, and she suddenly heels way over. We start up the engines quickly and pull her around. She ships water over the rails during the worst gusts. Everything is over in the course of a few minutes. Good experience to remember.

Later in the afternoon the wind blows briskly, and she heaves around a bit. My wife is seasick. I suggest, with a laugh, that 'this is fresh water. What will happen when you get out to sea?' But she is not in any state to comment on anything at all – she wants to be left alone! I say that it usually gets better, and find out that it is best I take a walk up on deck.

Some skyscrapers rise up on the horizon. They can be seen clearly above the low landscape – the Chicago skyline.

Chicago welcomes the ship. Photograph: Walter Kale

Most of what we have read about Chicago has been gangster stories. We have heard that it is a tough town. Assaults and all that sort of thing. (People are assaulted in Oslo, too, of course.)

An American journalist who has accompanied us from Montreal, Paul Galloway of the *Chicago Sun Times,* tells us a little about his city. Of course it has its darker aspects, just like all large cities all over the world, but in the last few years a lot has been improved in this area. He attributes this to Mayor Richard Daley, a well-known personality, almost legendary in American politics. He has run this city as mayor for twenty-three years – which is quite a record.

Paul, too, has fallen in love with our ship. He has sent long articles to his paper, which has followed us from day to day, so to speak. He writes about the young cadets, about the officers, about the crew, our wives, and is enthusiastic about Norwegians. He is a pleasant man, suitably modest, and nice to be with. One night he takes his courage in his hands and tells me his greatest desire: to sail with a square-rigger across the Atlantic Ocean, to sail with the *Radich* to Europe.

He could probably arrange to get leave from the newspaper. Besides which, his superiors could perhaps use material from the trip. There are a lot of possibilities. I explain to him about signing on, insurance, passport, and all the formalities. He is not frightened off by this. He would like to talk more about the matter.

While the sun goes down and brings the large buildings of the city into relief, we shorten sails and tack a dozen or so miles out in Lake Michigan. Radio stations have already reported our position, and the boats come out to meet us, in spite of the wind and high waves. The next morning I recognize a couple of them. By gosh, I think they have been out all night. With our topsails hoist, we sail in towards the harbor entrance. This is a man-made harbor, with the

IX

WE MEET THE PEOPLE AROUND THE LAKES

Four solemn young men under siege.
PHOTOGRAPH: STIG NÆSS

Tied up alongside Navy Pier in Chicago, with thousands of spectators.
PHOTOGRAPH: HEDRICH BLESSING

breakwater in a half-circle out towards the lake. Inside, more pleasure craft and fireboats are waiting for us. Before we reach the breakwater head, we lower and furl all sails. Above us, the usual planes and helicopters are buzzing. Norwegian wartime sailors, who have become Americans, come out in their own boat, flying a huge Norwegian flag. Inside the breakwater a fireboat comes up ahead of us and begins to spray out colorful streams of water, red, white and blue, the colors of both Norway and America. It's just that I cannot see a thing forward. We have to call him on the radio and ask him to move.

It is Sunday morning, August 1. It is almost ten o'clock. At that moment precisely we are to dock. We say no thank you to the two tugboats offering their assistance. It's best to manage alone, at any rate if there is a lot of room and the wind doesn't create problems. Port side is also the easier. The left controllable-pitch propeller sends the stern in towards the dock when we order astern. That is, she does as a rule, if she is in a good mood.

There is an unbelievable crowd in the harbor area. It is not possible to hear anything as we move slowly in towards the pier. Orders must be given in sign language. The boat sirens scream, people are yelling 'hurray,' big guns are saluting, and even the cars are tooting their horns.

We glide in to Navy Pier, a magnificent dock installation, which, in its time, belonged to the navy. Now it is more like a shore promenade. TV cameras are mounted on the nearby roofs and have a view of the enormous numbers of people. The reception committee, with Mayor Richard Daley himself at the fore, is standing on the pier. The gangway touches the shore at ten o'clock exactly. That makes us feel good. The band is standing there in ranks, in white naval uniforms. Ambassador Sommerfelt is there, with Consul General Riise and a lot of other people. Happily I see that Lasse Kolstad has also arrived. He is to collect money for the Friends of the *Christian Radich* Fund and make useful contacts here in the States.

And now we go ashore, Captain. The restful time is over, from now on you're 'scheduled' throughout your visit.

Microphones have been rigged up to loudspeakers on the dock, which can be heard all over the harbor area. I go ashore and meet the dignitaries. Both countries' national anthems are played. On deck, the boys are lined up and standing at attention. Colonel (Retired) Jack Reilly, the mayor's master of ceremonies, speaks first. He introduces the speakers in turn – first Daley, then the ambassador, and then me. It is difficult to thank them properly for the wonderful manner in which we are being received.

After the ceremony I invite the gentlemen on board, and we enjoy a glass of sherry in the saloon before the day's hectic program really begins.

We go through the program just once more – just to make sure. The City of Chicago, Office of the Mayor, had sent out a press release, two days previously, in which our youngsters were welcomed, and in which the extensive program that had been planned was repeated. The boys are going to be well taken care of.

Reilly is right. The boys are entertained, are spoiled with food, and get to see a number of interesting places, of which perhaps one of the most attractive is the Chicago police headquarters. The captain, as usual, is the man who gets to see the least.

The public has appeared in tremendous numbers. We are beginning to be used to this, to some extent, but we are constantly amazed at the interest in the Tall Ships and the patience people show in standing in line for hours in the hot sun. One couple, she very pregnant, stood there, waiting to come on board on arrival day. After awhile, she felt that now she had to get to the hospital. Before we left, I received a letter from the happy father of a girl, who will be given the name Christine, for the ship. We note down that a christening present should be sent when we get home.

'*C'mon, smile a little . . .*'
PHOTOGRAPH: STIG NÆSS

'*Big Chief.*'

The City of Chicago really 'puts on the dog' where honorary awards are concerned. On August 3 the captain, with his bride, is invited to city hall. The city council members are there, and the captain is made 'honorary citizen of the City of Chicago.' A long proclamation is read, in which the city thanks Norway for sending the *Christian Radich* to take part in the bicentennial celebration.

But everything has an end, including our visit to Chicago. On our last day we are visited by a delegation from Toledo, where we are to call later on. They are here in Chicago to 'spy.' They want to pick up ideas for their program. I am given a sketch with the height of some high-voltage cables we have to pass under in Toledo Harbor. It looks OK, and I don't think anything more about it.

When we were in Montreal two men from Muskegon had come on a visit. Where the devil is Muskegon? They realize that I am not quite aware of what they want, and they explain. The two gentlemen talk fast and a lot: they want the *Radich* to make a call at Muskegon – which is located on the eastern side of Lake Michigan. – Not on your life; we don't have time! Our program is too packed already. In addition to the original program, we have included a short visit to Grand Haven, just south of Muskegon. This had been arranged in Bermuda, where we were visited by representatives of this little town, who came for that specific purpose.

The Muskegon people won't take no for an answer. They give me an Indian headdress that I must promise to wear when I sail into the harbor. Sail into the harbor? I have just said that we don't have time!

The end of the whole affair is that our departure from Chicago is pushed ahead ten hours. This gives us time to sail into Muskegon's harbor, turn, and sail out again. You've never seen such gratitude! The two gentlemen return home happily with the great news. I can only shake my head in wonder.

In the evening of August 3 we make ready for departure. Again, thousands of people who want to bid us farewell. When we arrived, three days previously, it was said that about 65,000 people were in the harbor area to receive us. You have to take these figures with a grain of salt, but one thing is sure: there were a lot of people. How many have come down here to the pier tonight I don't know, but it is very moving. We still don't understand why they have done it. At home they would think we were telling stories if we were to describe our experiences. There they stand in the light of the harbor lamps and wave goodbye, all our known and unknown friends. How can we thank you for all of your friendliness and hospitality? You have made us feel at home among you.

We back out from the pier. It's blowing hard out on the lake. The wind carries the last Goodbyes and God-bless-yous as the pilot turns her around on course for the harbor exit.

Goodbye, Chicago!

I have an old gentleman as pilot. Not to disparage any of the many pilots we have had, but Captain Morgan is special. His name is really Morgan Howell, but he suggests that we use first names, he is more used to that. And I don't mind at all. So we call each other Captain Morgan and Captain Kjell. He is used to style, and Captain Morgan is really in style. He is seventy-six years old and should have retired. I don't know the rules for pensioning off pilots on the Great Lakes, and Captain Morgan would rather talk about something else, I realize. He is determined to sail to the bitter end. He has the pilots' Golden Ticket, the certificate for the whole East Coast of the United States.

A long life on lake ships has brought him into contact with a great many Norwegians. He sailed for a long period under a Norwegian captain, for whom he has the greatest respect. Another Norwegian for whom Captain Morgan has great respect is Max Manus. He has read about Manus' escapades during the Second World War, and Max Manus has a faithful admirer in the old pilot. I must promise to greet Max Manus for Captain Morgan when I return to Norway.

The little city of 4,000 inhabitants, lying in a natural harbor here on the east side of Lake Michigan, has an Indian name. Two breakwaters protect the entrance to Muskegon. The entrance is a narrow channel, lined with stones on both sides. We are lucky, have a westerly wind that allows us to sail into port with topsails flying.

Four thousand inhabitants? The number must be double that, at least on this day: They are lined up along the channel shores again, thousands of Americans who shout welcome to one single sailing ship. Captain Morgan is at the helm himself, and he is enjoying himself like a little boy at that big wheel. I put on my Indian headdress, as they said I should, the two gentlemen who persuaded us to sail here.

When I see the enthusiasm shown by all of these people, I'm glad we have come. Our White Swan preens herself in the admiration of the inland population. Again, unknown friends to wave farewell to.

Twelve nautical miles south of Muskegon is Grand Haven, an apparently sleepy town of 12,000 inhabitants. The U.S. Coast Guard is 100 years old this year. This organization, whose presence is felt in so many areas – sea rescues, safety at sea, communications, weather forecasting, etc. – has 2,000 men stationed on the Great Lakes. Rear Admiral Gracey is head of this force, and he has invited us to Grand Haven to take part in the birthday party. He has his headquarters there, and we arrange a reception on board for specially invited guests.

This is quite an event in this little town. The ladies come dressed to the teeth, with newly-set hair and long dresses. We have done ourselves proud with goodies in both solid and fluid form.

And then the rains come! But people have gotten all dressed up and have been looking forward to this for several days, so just let it rain! Large, cold raindrops splash down on bare female shoulders, which gradually become bumpy with goose pimples and take on the color of skimmed milk. Our white uniforms get a little dingy around the edges. We don't have room for the guests below, so we hold out on the deck.

Finally the rain stops. The admiral and I exchange nice speeches, I am given a

70

'Christian Radich' as the gulls see her.
PHOTOGRAPH: SHOSTAL ASSOCIATES

souvenir gift from the visit, and the guests go happily ashore. Slightly frozen, but they have been to a party on the Tall Ship.

We must sail on. The youngsters have been to a fair in the vicinity. At the last possible moment they come galloping on board, ten minutes late. For once we disregard it. Maybe the reason was a few pretty girls up the road a piece. One should be understanding about this kind of thing.

We get a Coast Guard cutter to pull us away from the dock, order 'ahead' on the engine, and with Captain Morgan at the wheel we leave Grand Haven. A few hundred miles north, about half a dozen by sea, is our next port of call, Duluth, named for a man of French ancestry, who hunted all over this area.

We sail north on Lake Michigan, through Mackinac Strait. During the night we go up the narrow canal towards Sault Sainte Marie. We have pea-soup-thick fog for a few minutes. The narrow canal does not allow any leeway for maneuvering. It is forbidden to anchor, nor can a ship be tied up to the canal banks. Fortunately, the fog disappears.

Daylight appears, and we sail on our engine along shores where the leafy trees hang out over the water, as in a jungle. We can see cosy little houses through the

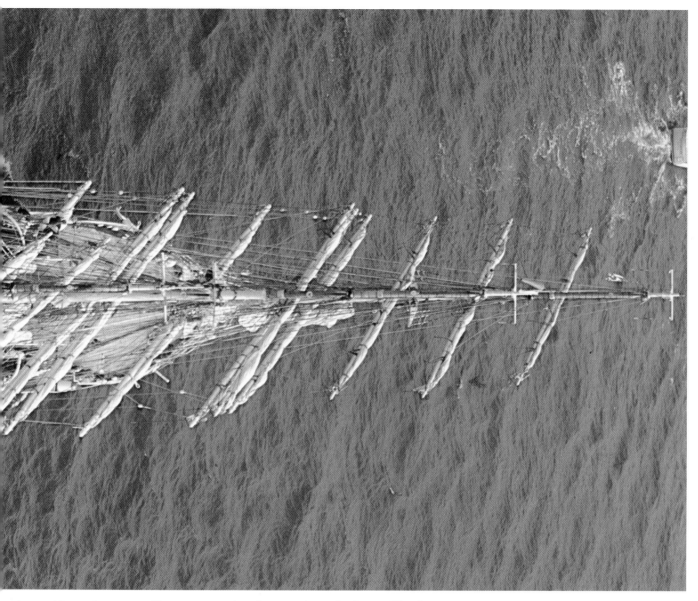

trees. Above the swamplike open terrain, the morning mist hangs like frosty breath and reminds us that summer is passing.

The two locks at Sault Sainte Marie are 'peanuts' for us lock veterans. Pleasant lock crews see to it that we get through quickly, ahead of the waiting traffic.

Then we sail into Lake Superior. The *Christian Radich* is the first square-rigger on this lake, 601 feet above the mean sea level, we have heard. Lake Superior is deep and cold and known for its wildness during the autumn storms. As recently as the previous year a laker had sunk, with thirty-two men on board. No survivors.

We have good weather all the way. We sail, too. The wind is favorable, and for the first time people can see a square-rigger spread her wings up here. One lovely evening actor Lasse Kolstad gets the boys together on the fo'c'sle to entertain them. Lasse sits down on the capstan with his guitar and gives the boys an unforgettable evening. He is in love with the ship, himself, and is well acquainted with her from the *Windjammer* movie.

Again we have plenty of time before our next port of call. The last night we make our way westward at slow speed. Again the small boats come out to greet us. One of the first is a Norwegian-built boat, a motorsailer of the Troll type, built at Askvik Boatyard in Os, near Bergen. Riveted hull, thirty feet, constructed as a fishing boat. A huge Norwegian flag is hoisted in our honor.

Captain Morgan and I lay the operations plan. We are to be alongside the pier at 10:00 A.M. exactly, on August 9. Using small sails we ease toward the entrance, lower sails just before the canal, and pass under the lifting bridge. Aerial Bridge, height, 150 feet, it says on the chart. Twenty feet higher than the mainmast. A shudder goes up from the thousands of onlookers when it looks as though the mast hits the bridge.

Captain Morgan is at the helm. We have gradually come to work well together, and we understand each other. Again, we manage without the tugboat, and at ten o'clock we lie with our port side alongside a flag-decorated pier. This time too she turns her stern the right way.

In the middle of the mass of people on the dockside is the speakers' stand. Margrethe and I are brought forward and placed in full view of everyone up there, along with the welcoming committee. Again, speeches and proclamations, from both Duluth and her twin city of Superior, in Wisconsin.

Our energetic vice-consul, Miss Elsie Melbye, is one of the driving forces behind the program here in Duluth. Like so many people in Minnesota and Wisconsin, she is of Norwegian or Scandinavian descent. A lot of work has gone into arranging this program, which will keep us busy during the next four days. A hotel room is put at our disposal. It is nice to get away from the cramped cabin for a few hours.

The icebreaker *Mackinac,* which is so wide that she never leaves the lakes, is tied up ahead of us. The city announces Maritime Heritage Week – and people come by the tens of thousands down to the harbor to look at the ships. The restaurants in the city do a great deal of business, and the camera stores run out of film. The hotels are overfilled, and people have to travel long distances to find a place to rest their heads. Some of them have traveled 600 miles in order to set foot on the deck of the *Christian Radich.* A heavy rainstorm with hail surprises the long line of people one day. They are soaked completely through but don't move out of their places in line. We don't feel right when we close down in the evenings and see the hundreds who have been waiting in vain, but we must have a chance to eat our meals, clean up, and get some sleep.

A car is lent to us, with automatic gearshift – a huge beast of a car in which Margrethe and I are to try to get away for a couple of hours. I start it, and, aside from beginner's difficulties in finding the hand brake, things go pretty well. On the return trip we get on a one-way street – coming from the wrong way. Counter-traffic and full traffic stop! But a Norwegian flag is hanging on the aerial, and an approaching policeman realizes that we have come from the Tall Ship. He guides us out and waves encouragingly. I would rather forget Margrethe's comments.

Duluth harbor is in the process of great expansion, since shipping is on the rise again on the lakes. The grain loading goes on rapidly, and boat after boat fills its belly at the large silos. The old 'whalebacks,' ships with a somewhat cylindrical-shaped hull (like a whale's back) and steam engines, trafficed the lakes in the tough old days. One of these boats is now used as a museum, and the cadets study the ship and hear how shipping has developed down through the years.

One evening a ball is given for the youngsters. Young people today do not appear to like dances in the old-fashioned sense of the word. I stand and watch the young men approach with their partners, past parents almost bursting with pride. They applaud, and the girls blush. Our boys look mostly as if they would prefer to disappear through the floor. The orchestra begins to play, but it takes a long time before the young people dare go out on the floor. Finally they thaw out and dare to go over to the girls' side, to ask the ones they have picked out to dance.

Oslo's city emblem flies from the bowsprit.
PHOTOGRAPH: WILLIAM RHYINS

Arrival at Duluth, escorted by a Norwegian-built motor-sailer with a huge Norwegian flag in her crosstree. PHOTOGRAPH: CHARLES CURTIS

The four days come to an end, and we must go on. This is a poignant farewell, with a good many 'be seeing you's,' although we really think that there is a small chance of this. We sail in the evening on August 12, and use the staysails and engine out of the channel. All sails are set on the way out into Superior, to the joy of innumerable photographers on the water and ashore. We have said goodbye to Captain Morgan in Duluth. He had hoped to pilot us farther, but he had to go out on another job.

Our pilot is named Jack Lion, known as one of the best on the lakes in his profession.

The sun goes down behind the hills, and with Duluth lying in its shadow, sends its last rays onto our sails. It must make the ship a beautiful sight for those who escort us some distance on our travels.

X

THE MASS MEDIA ACCOMPANY THE SHIP

We are proud of our flag, which flies from the gaff. PHOTOGRAPH: FINN BERGAN

Friday the thirteenth – the day of the week and the date that, together, can mean great misfortune – we spend on our way to Sault Sainte Marie. Nothing happens.

On Saturday morning we go through the lower-the-masts operation again. With our experience, this is now done in two hours. We are to pass under a bridge that is only 120 feet high. We do it underway while the weather is good. At 11:55 A.M. we enter the McArthur Lock. The people of Sault Sainte Marie have asked us to stop at their city. We have a fair amount of time and lie a couple of hours alongside the dock, so that people can see the ship at close quarters. In the late afternoon we cast off and run with the current down the canals. The topgallant masts are raised again and the rigging adjusted. At sunset we anchor for the night at the northern end of Lake Huron.

During the whole of the eventful trip in the United States we have had press people, TV people, and radio people accompanying us, up to twelve guests at a time. They sit in the saloon, and our patience is tried, now and again. Kilometer after kilometer of film has been taken of the ship and her crew. The youngsters have become accustomed to being in the limelight and appear to enjoy being filmed. Tough reporters, who are used to seeing rough stuff, seem to calm down on board, relaxing from their otherwise pressured rhythm. I answer questions, talk sailing ships, juvenile problems, what we think of America and the people there, why I am a captain on a sailing ship, etc. The reporters write long articles about their journey with the *Christian Radich*, even though their trip may just be between two harbors, where the sailing time can be only a few hours long.

Our Information Service in New York, which has picked out the reporters, has done a good job of getting hold of the right people.

The ship is also used for a number of other purposes in promoting information about Norway. In New York the *Christian Radich* was definitely the most talked-about vessel. We have found three main reasons for this:

1. The ship became famous after the *Windjammer* film.
2. The young crew have completely charmed the Americans.
3. There has been competent picking of the TV teams and reporters. On July 3 there was a forty-five-minute program by the TV stations in New York, recorded on board our ship.

On the busy Fourth of July our ship was the star of a fifteen-minute program. This is good and inexpensive publicity for Norway. It didn't cost us a cent. Everywhere we have been, ever since then, there has been copy on the radio, on TV, and in the papers every day, and in great quantities.

I sit on the quarterdeck this evening, while at anchor in Lake Huron, and discuss the power of mass media with our guests, who are professionals in the field.

Americans watch TV a lot. They are good radio listeners. The radio is always turned on in their cars, to and from their jobs. During free time at home the TV always seems to be turned on. How they ever have time to read papers, I don't know, but newspaper sales are way up, at any rate. We come back to this with the Tall Ships, the parade in New York, and visits to other cities.

Our guests emphasize that this is one of the best things that has happened to the Americans in a long time. This particular element has roused the greatest interest of all the arrangements. They are proud of the fact that so many countries have sent ships to the U.S. as guests, during the bicentennial. The mass media coverage of the sailing ships' visit has been tremendous. Naturally, it is not just the *Christian Radich* that has been given a good press. In the discussion of the different ships, a little bit or a great deal is written about the country they come from. They also write about the 'spirit of the sea,' about the helpfulness at sea, the solidarity.

Our friend Paul Galloway, from Chicago, expressed it this way:

'The parade of sailing ships in New York was the single event that was the most impressive and gripping for the Americans on the Fourth of July. The reaction among people was unexpected, and it is difficult to explain, but it was very real, and was felt all over the country. As a journalist I had the opportunity to read most of what has been written about the bicentennial in newspapers from all over the U.S.A. Almost without exception, both the reporters and the people who were interviewed referred to the parade of the Tall Ships. For some people, these ships symbolize a bond, roots of their past. For others, the ships' simplicity and beauty roused hopes and visions for the future.'

The whole fleet has received a copy of a letter that President Gerald Ford sent to the man who has the responsibility for Operation Sail 1976, Ambassador Emil Mosbacher, Jr. The letter is dated: The White House, Washington, 3 July 1976.

The President concluded more or less in these words: 'In gathering large sailing ships from other countries, you are also emphasizing the international solidarity and goodwill we need, and which we consider essential to the efforts to give our country a peaceful third century...'

The President was right. The whole Operation Sail has been a great success.

The next morning is as beautiful as a dream. With the sunrise, there is a nice little northerly breeze that blows away the remnants of the blanket of fog that covers the small swampy stretches ashore during the night. The summer has reached its peak up here on the lakes.

We weigh anchor under sail. The crew is fully trained now, so there is no problem with an offshore wind. We sail south across Lake Huron. We skim down along the shore on the starboard side, so that people can see the ship –

Evening on Lake Superior, 184 meters (601 feet) above sea level.

there are constant requests for this. We have a radio reporter along who sends out regular reports on our doings directly over the air.

The next morning we pass Port Huron, on our way out this time. The river current is very strong. We sweep along at about fourteen to sixteen knots absolute speed where it is narrowest. A large fleet of pleasure craft 'are lying neck and neck' with us. The pilot suggests the westerly lane out to Lake Saint Clair. We sail in idyllic surroundings, past lovely houses with large gardens, where it looks as though people are able to enjoy life.

Out in the sunny haze over Lake Saint Clair a couple of thousand small boats are waiting. Speedboats with unforgivable amounts of horsepower stir up the quiet surface, so that a couple of the smaller boats capsize.

The fleet appears to grow as we approach Detroit. An odd, ferrylike boat with garlands of flowers and flowerpots along the railing is manned with a Dixieland orchestra. They come close, and over the loudspeakers on the cabin roof can be heard our national anthem in jazz tempo. This is the first time we have heard that. Afterwards they salute us with their straw hats. We enter the Detroit River. On both sides factories and power plants begin to appear. The river forms the boundary with Canada, and it is obvious that the American side is the more developed.

As we approach the city more boats join the fleet, including large sight-seeing ferries, which have changed their regular routes for the occasion.

We are slightly early. And that shouldn't happen on an official visit. You have to give your hosts a chance to get finished so that they can receive you.

Even though we delay as much as se can, we slide alongside the dock at 6:15 P.M., three-quarters of an hour early. We blame the strong favorable current, but there is no excuse. We offer our apologies, but events prove that it doesn't really matter: the city's mayor has expressed his regrets at the last minute and left town. There evidently has been a demonstration by young people a few days earlier. So our reception is somewhat improvised, but the whole affair is smoothed over.

Because of the above-mentioned demonstrations, extra police forces have been called in. The city fathers are scared stiff that something will happen to our youngsters. For this reason there is a twenty-four-hour police guard in the harbor area during our stay there. A police boat patrols the river all around the clock.

Weary 'ambassador' for Norway.

As is the case in all of the cities on the lakes, the boys become good friends with the police. They exchange souvenirs. Our T-shirts are very popular. The boys are given police shirts, clubs, and even handcuffs. We have to put an end to business, as the stocks of belaying pins from the boatswain's store are radically reduced.

During all the activities ashore one or more of the adult crew members go along. The boys are under supervision at every moment. Some of them think that this gets to be more than enough 'babying,' but they realize why it's necessary and that we who are responsible for them want to get them home in good condition.

In Detroit, as has been the case in many other places, the youngsters are invited home to American families, usually those of Norwegian extraction. Sometimes we let the cadets stay overnight with their hosts. They don't mind this at all, obviously. From a hot mess deck, with hammocks and forty-three shipmates, they come into a home, as a rule a fairly wealthy home by our standards, are waited on, allowed to stay up later than 10:00 P.M., and are given a large bed with sheets and all the comforts in their own room.

Outside of Detroit is Greenfield Village, with the Henry Ford Museum. For youth interested in machinery, it is a dream come true to see this. They can see, at first hand, the first technical inventions with which this versatile man enriched his era.

General Motors has its kingdom here, and the *Christian Radich* has a GM main engine. This is interesting: even sailing ships use GM! The publicity people in the large company swarm on board and shoot movies and take stills.

Our friend Bjørn Kvisgaard has arrived from New York, and, with characteristic efficiency, he has made arrangements under the auspices of the Export Council of Norway. 'Soft selling,' he says. American customers and potential customers, industrial leaders, politicians, and anyone else who has influence from which we can benefit, are invited on board and served Norwegian food and Norwegian drinks – very popular parties wherever Bjørn arranges them.

So we're not in the U.S. just to have a good time. The exploitation value of the ship for the Norwegian Information Service and the Export Council of Norway is incalculable – cheap, effective, favorable publicity.

Thursday, August 19, 10:00 A.M. Ship's departure.

> Present at pier, city officials,
> committee, and press.

They're all standing there, when we leave. People from the Mayor's Office, the bicentennial committee, all the newspapers, and TV. In our log we can write up one more visit in the column under 'successful.'

Just six hours from Detroit to Toledo. This is beginning to be somewhat hectic. You have to readjust mentally to a new reception, to say something that won't just be a repetition of what has already been said many times. The chairman of the OPSAIL-76 committee in Toledo accompanies us from Detroit.

I get out the sketches we were given in Chicago by Toledo's 'spy.' There's something here that isn't quite right. On the chart are marked some high-voltage cables that are stretched across the harbor entrance, height above normal water level, 125 feet. Our mainmast is 130 feet high. The sketch from Chicago says that the cables are stretched at a height of 145 feet.

Ask the Coast Guard. That's the solution – they know everything. 'Toledo Coast Guard, this is the Norwegian sail training ship *Christian Radich,* call sign Lima Juliet Lima Mike; do you hear me? Over.' Oh yes, he hears us. But he says that, according to his information, the cable height is that on the chart, 125 feet. I call up the harbor office, but they won't say anything beyond what the Coast Guard has said.

The Christian Radich's figurehead, Christina.
PHOTOGRAPH: ROBERT MEYER

We know that thousands of people are waiting along the shore to watch our proud windjammer arrive at the ceremonial pier, way up in the harbor basin. The chairman of the committee is called. 'Do you understand my dilemma?' I ask. 'Yes, of course, Captain.' 'Well,' I say, 'find me a pier way out in the inlet before we reach the high-tension pylons. We'll lie there until I have a paper saying that these cables are high enough to allow our rigging to pass.'

But the reception committee, minus the chairman, is standing and waiting for us, up the river. What now?

Quick telephone conversation, quick decision. The committee chairman fixes things. The committee orders two buses. We pile in, and arrive a couple of hours late for the reception ceremony in a huge warehouse, decorated for the occasion. They return home disappointed, those who had hoped to see this fata morgana, this ghost ship, which they had read so much about. They just get a glimpse of the crew, which jumps informally out of two buses.

The press is not terribly nice the next day. I try to explain why we couldn't take the chance.

Late last evening we were given the paper I had asked for, which means that the charts and the information from the Coast Guard are not acceptable as to accuracy. This means in practice that the power company that owns the cables is right and that the official figures are wrong. We cast off and move in to our ceremonial dock. I pretend that I'm not looking up as we pass under the cables carrying several thousand nasty volts.

The boys sling their hammocks on deck during their off watch and take out their guitars. Could life be better?   PHOTOGRAPHS: FINN BERGAN

The extremely energetic members of the reception committee drive themselves and us very hard. They have the advantage in that they have been waiting for this a long time. Expectations have been building up, and now all of this stored-up energy is to be released. The guests won't have a chance to be bored.

For us, the situation is a bit different. We wouldn't mind winding down a few notches. But the knowledge that this will only happen just once in a lifetime, all of these experiences, makes us try to absorb all the impressions, collect experiences. Movies and pictures will be taken out again, in a quieter time, at home. 'Do you remember this? Remember that time?'

In Toledo we are given what must be the world's finest hotel rooms. The Commodore Perry Hotel has a roof apartment with a gigantic balcony and with a private elevator, of course, and with a bar as long as a Norwegian Saturday-night party – with three double bedrooms furnished with ankle-deep rugs and innumerable color television sets. The only trouble is, we don't have time to enjoy our luxury. We fall into bed at midnight, and the next morning, early, we are on the go again.

Through the gatherings at the home of the port's commodore, the local yacht clubs, and on board, we again gain a circle of friends. The friendliness and the hospitality constantly amaze us; we cannot really become accustomed to it. 'What have we done to deserve all this?' I often tell myself that we must retain a sense of humbleness and gratitude because we are among those enjoying the privilege of experiencing America and the people here in this manner. We are, of course, quite aware that we are not seeing all aspects of this society. We do not see the slums, the poverty, and the hopelessness experienced by many people. We see the sunny side, the nice things.

But we are guests at their 200th anniversary. We Norwegians also put on our best clothes and take people into the best parlor when guests come to our house.

Sunday, August 22, 1976.

A fleet of yachts will escort the *Christian Radich* to the harbor light to bid farewell and safe journey – 7:00 A.M.

And that is just what a fleet of yachts do on Sunday morning. People turn out

at 5:00 A.M. to escort us out with their boats. The tugboat pulls us out from the dock, and we are on our way out of the harbor with the many bridges. These bridges are a nightmare for me. On the way in it wasn't so bad. We were running against the current and could reduce speed and have full control over our steering until the bridges opened. Some of them are swing bridges, while others split in the middle, and the roadbed opens like a double door. They open at the last minute – the absolutely last second, I have the impression.

As far as I can see, there is no coordination of when the bridges are to open. The various authorities that own the bridges have their people in the operator's compartment, and these guys decide when the bridge is to be opened, when a ship gives the signal that it wants to pass.

On the way out of the harbor, we are running with the current, and it is impossible to stop. We just have to let her go. It looks as though the bridge operators are extraordinarily slow on this early Sunday morning. In one spot we go close to shore in order to have vertical clearance enough for an aerial cable. The wires hang between two masts on the shores of the river and are thus lowest in the middle. We turn hard astarboard and line up for the bridge opening. Even the pilot is worried. The bridge just doesn't move. We can't see the red light that means that traffic is stopping, either, and now it is right at the last minute. Our whistle again gives the signal that we are on our way out and 'please open the bridge.' I 'take off the way' of the ship. Not too much astern, or she will lose her steerageway.

The current is carrying us steadily closer. Has the bridge operator gone to sleep? Is he in the bathroom? Why the hell doesn't he open the bridge?

Finally. Finally we hear a bell ring. A red light shows that traffic has been stopped. The last car drives at a snail's pace across the bridge in first gear before the boom can go down and the bridge is lifted. I tell the pilot that I sure don't envy him his job.

A slight westerly breeze makes it possible to set sails out on Lake Erie. It is hazy a few hours after sunrise. We do a few knots southeastward along the marked channel. Lake Erie is the shallowest of the lakes. Because of this, in stormy weather choppy waves can build up rapidly and can be dangerous for small boats. We hear that *Erawan,* the ship we almost ran over during the start from Bermuda, was in trouble here on Lake Erie just a couple of weeks ago. The *Erawan* was on her way to Chicago to earn money carrying passengers.

Some of the yachts blow their horns in farewell and return to Toledo. Some new ones appear from the east, from our next port, Cleveland. The fleet grows in size as we sail along the route marked by buoys. On starboard side we have Cedar Point, a center for sports and recreation, where the boys have spent a day. To port we see the Commodore Perry monument, which is floodlighted during the night. Commodore Perry was a sea hero who beat the English in a naval battle on Lake Erie.

We lower and furl all sails just before the Cleveland harbor entrance. The harbor has no natural protection, but it is sheltered by a long breakwater, the longest man-made breakwater in the world, we are told. The U.S. Army has an airport in the harbor area, and a squadron of eight khaki-colored helicopters flies over us in beautiful formation. From the shore comes the sound of cannon salutes and cheers. Again, enthusiastic masses of people who have come to greet what for them is a rare guest and to welcome her, a guest from far away in the Old World.

Again, thousands on the dock. Here at Cleveland they have had the headquarters for all OPSAIL-76 committees on the Great Lakes. In addition to us, they are visited by two smaller schooners, one of them Polish. The *Christian Radich* slides in toward a flag-festooned pier. Mayor Perk and his entourage come aboard before I have time to go to the gangway and receive them properly. On the quarterdeck microphones are rigged up, and again there are welcoming speeches and speeches of thanks carried out to the listeners. Gifts are given, and as usual I have to have help to carry everything down to the saloon afterwards.

Cleveland, the City of Woods, has about 4.5 million inhabitants. The leaders of the city are in the middle of preparations for elections. Mayor Perk takes time, even so, to get away from the office and be our host during our stay. Things like that happen in this amazing, great country.

Cleveland has had her ration of crime, like all of the large American cities. We are not to go out on the streets after dark, so we don't. Our time is usually completely programmed, with little or no possibility of investigating the city's nightlife.

The city is called the City of Woods. In the old days there were great forests here. There still are large 'green lungs' in the city urban area. I can see this clearly one day, when the mayor invites me to take a helicopter trip over the city. We fly in two of the choppers that came out to meet us. There are eight men in all, and we sit there comfortably with headphones on, while our hosts describe the scenery passing beneath us. Cleveland is known for her industry. Tools and machine-parts production are the dominant industries. The city also has hospitals with supermodern equipment and a worldwide reputation. Researchers from all over the world work here.

The two pilots land their choppers with great military precision. In thanks for the superb excursion, I invite the crews of both helicopters on board.

One afternoon we have a visit by a police sergeant from Grand Haven. He had been on board just a short while when we visited his hometown. He has brought along thirty-six police shirts, which he and his colleagues have understood the youngsters to be interested in. In return, he wants to buy *Radich* shirts. He has brought along his daughter, who is ten to twelve years old and suffering from an incurable disease. They have been told by the doctor that she will not live more than a year.

She wants to see our ship. She does, and her father is given the *Radich* shirts – free.

Our energetic vice-consul, Henry Lucas, is an important 'wheel' on the bicentennial committee. He is a lawyer, but he lets his practice get along on its own when the *Radich* is visiting. He has worked one year on coordinating OPSAIL-76 events on the Great Lakes.

Meetings with committees from other cities, trips in conjunction with the bicentennial – in addition to his job itself, this takes both time and energy. How many busy bees have been working to make this 200th anniversary a success nobody knows.

One day I have to collect money from the bank. More than $4,000 for the ship's cash box. I ask Henry where the bank is and whether he can get hold of transportation for me if it is too far to walk.

'Walk?' He looks at me inquiringly. 'Walk? Oh, no. I'll drive you, but not alone.'

Now I look at him very questioningly.

'I'll arrange for a police escort.'

'Oh?'

'Well, you see you mustn't walk around with so much money on you. Somebody might want to share it with you.'

Innocent Norwegians. Country boy in the big city.

Henry puts me in the front seat of his car, with an armed policeman on my right. A police car drives ahead of us. Just like a cops-and-robbers movie. In front of the bank, the police car stops, the driver gets out and looks around. He comes over to us. 'Pull up behind me and double park,' he says. We do this, and then we go into the bank, where I have to be introduced to the staff. Two of the mates have come along, just incidentally, and the people behind the windows are pleased to have a talk with the Tall Ship people. A special room for counting money. An armed guard, whom I ask to help me count a couple of the piles of bills. When we get back on the ship I go on board with a policeman in front of me and one behind. Not until I have set foot on deck do they consider that their job is finished. They are invited on board and are given some souvenirs for their children.

On Wednesday, August 25, we back out from the dock, and in a light, offshore breeze, we set all sails. We wave farewell to the people of Cleveland, the City of Woods.

We have fog in the evening. The radar isn't quite in order. We have plenty of time, and I anchor for the night in the harbor of Erie, the city that has given the lake its name. We are offered a berth at the dock, but I would rather have a quiet evening, and I try to explain this. Everyone on board is worn out, and quiet settles over the ship very early. The last thing I hear, before the sandman takes over, is the youngster on watch, who is pacing the quarterdeck above my cabin to keep warm in the clammy night fog.

Before people have waked up ashore the next morning, we weigh anchor. As we start up, fire breaks out in the radar power converter. A fire extinguisher makes short work of the flames. So now we have no radar! This had to happen when the fog is as thick as a blanket, of course.

PHOTOGRAPH: CHARLES CURTIS

PHOTOGRAPH: ROBERT MEYER

We shorten sail. Three of the boys are aloft to furl the foreroyal. PHOTOGRAPH: FINN BERGAN

Using the excellent communications network here on the lakes, I soon make contact with our agent. He writes down the type and series number of the power converter and promises to meet us with a spare at the next harbor, provided it can be found in the States.

The sun finally manages to break through the fog.

I understand that our guests from TV and the papers would like to see the youngsters in action aloft. OK, we'll try to break the record. The record? Yes, from furled sails, with the crew on deck, until all sails are set, we have heard that this particular ship's record is nine minutes. Bring out the stopwatch. The cadets realize that now they're going to make history, if they're quick enough. OK, boys. You'll have to work fast. No dallying in the ratlines, but be careful!

'Man stations, ready to go aloft.' Whoosh, they're ready in the ratlines. 'Aloft and set all sails.' The stopwatch starts. The boys know that the cameras are following them, and I notice that this is good inspiration. Besides, they're out to set a new record. The last royal is set after seven minutes, forty seconds. The boys cheer and really feel good. So do I, actually. This exhibition is an indication of a thoroughly trained crew.

Buffalo is at the eastern end of Lake Erie and our next port of call. A strong current runs here at the beginning of the Niagara River. We have to turn the ship around at a narrow part of the river. We just manage it, and this time we are exactly on time. At 1900 hours she is alongside. Our dock is a new construction, and the *Christian Radich* has the honor of being the first ship alongside. Mayor Stanley M. Makowski comes on board, along with Commander de Castro and all members of the bicentennial and OPSAIL committees.

De Castro has had a brilliant idea. He has found out that Margrethe and I have not had a single day off on this honeymoon. Because of this, we are scheduled to disappear from the world for a day. He places a huge Cadillac and chauffeur at our disposal. The driver's name is Ann; she is a navy reservist, blond and well-built.

Half an hour after our arrival reception has begun, Margrethe and I are chased ashore and into the car, which takes us up to Niagara Falls. There we are checked into a hotel, driven to a restaurant for dinner, expenses paid, and Ann says that she will come back to get us the following afternoon. I change into civilian clothes, and now we are tourists, along with all of the other visitors.

Niagara Falls is a place to which newlyweds and tourists come. Why newlyweds come there I don't know, but I can understand why tourists do. The masses of water that rush out over the edge and end in a thundering chaos of foam all the way down are incredibly powerful. We visit the Niagara Falls Museum and look at the amazing craft that daredevils have used through the years for their journeys out over the falls. People who either have made bets or were trying to prove something to themselves have allowed themselves to be shut into a barrel and sent over the falls – daring men and women, who would not be welcomed as clients by an insurance company.

Ann arrives, as agreed upon, in the afternoon. She has just brought a gang of the youngsters, who had been to see the famous falls, back to the ship. The rest of the cadets are to come up tomorrow.

Buffalo is our last port in the United States. It has been a busy time, ever since the coast of New England rose on the horizon. There have been innumerable and intense impressions. We need time to absorb everything we have experienced, to analyze the material, and to find some sort of contour, content, form. A few months from now we will undoubtedly have an overview and be able to answer the question they are going to ask back home: 'What did you do in America?'

We wave goodbye to Buffalo on August 29, at sunset. Odd to think that now our hectic life is finished. Now we can begin to taper off, back to normal.

We have a quiet evening, lying at anchor off Port Colborne. The Welland

Canal has been closed one whole day because of a strike, and traffic has built up on both sides. We have to wait our turn. This is just as well, because that way we get a good night's sleep and can run the canal in daylight.

At six-thirty the next morning we weigh anchor and enter the canal. This is my last chance to take the ship through the canal without the aid of a pilot. 'Could you please just be around?' 'Certainly, Sir.' The pilot hovers around, and I have fun, taking the ship in and out of the locks.

In the evening we anchor off Port Welland on Lake Ontario, where we were delayed on our trip in. The next morning we are to cross to the other side of the lake, to Canada.

St. Lawrence Seaway has an impressive lock system that connects the Great Lakes with the sea. From Montreal we entered a canal system with locks that 'lift' the ships up to the lakes. Highest of all is Lake Superior, with her 601 feet above average sea level. Here we are going through one of the sluices in the Welland Canal, between Lake Ontario and Lake Erie.

PHOTOGRAPH: ARNSTEIN BUGGE

XI

OUT TO SEA AGAIN

Toronto, a known and loved name for many Norwegians, from the last war. The hangars from war days, built in connection with 'Little Norway,' are still standing on the old airfield. I think that many of our airmen from that period would have difficulties in recognizing the city itself. The core city is new, modern, made out of glass and concrete, and cold. Everything is big. Modern sculptures, the buildings – it gives me a feeling of suffocation.

But it's clean here, heaven knows. Thoroughly clean and sterile.

When we put alongside the dock, a few people are waiting for us. 'Are we home now, Captain?' one of the boys jokes. You're right, I think to myself. It is in the U.S.A. that our beloved ship attracts the greatest attention and exerts her greatest appeal.

My friend Bjørn Kvisgaard is on the spot again, to be adviser for his colleague in Ottawa on a minicruise we are to take out from Toronto, under the auspices of the Export Council of Norway.

Toronto has built a gigantic, towerlike building with TV aerials on the top. The world's highest, they say. We are told that the city has ambitions – it is in sharp competition with the capital city of the country, Ottawa.

On Friday, September 3, Margrethe leaves. She is to drive with Bjørn to Montreal and fly home. Her job is waiting. It was crowded with two in my little cabin, but, heaven knows, it certainly is empty when she is gone.

We sail in the evening. A quiet farewell to Toronto. There has not been the same sense of hurry about these days, but then we have not been invited for any great occasion; this is just a courtesy visit.

We are beginning to center all our thoughts on the trip home. Now we sail directly to Montreal, make the vessel ready for sea, and then we're off for Europe. It is about time. Autumn is approaching. Last year we sailed from New York on September 12. This year we are a little earlier, but the Atlantic usually starts getting autumn-peevish about this time. We used thirty-two days to Falmouth last year, but then we were sailing without the use of her engine.

The next day the fore- and main-topgallant masts are lowered for the last time on this trip. We are to pass under the bridges in the Saint Lawrence Seaway. Again we see the beautiful Thousand Islands. The summer homes are beginning to empty. In a lot of places the shutters have been put on the windows, and the place is 'laid up' for the winter.

I do not like the evening's weather forecast. It's blowing too much. We are to put in to and out of locks with the wind abeam. She is drifting too much. I want to wait until daylight before passing through the locks. We anchor for the night. Before the rooster crows, we weigh anchor on September 5. The last day in the seaway. As we turn out of the last lock all the way down by Montreal, I wonder if I will ever again sail on the Great Lakes.

We are the richer for having been there, on the lakes, for six weeks. In the middle of North America, we have found thousands of friends. We have been guests in a country that accepted so many of our countrymen when times were hard at home in Norway. These people have left their mark on their new country. Along with immigrants from other European countries, who fled from hunger and a degrading way of life, they have built a society where personal freedom has been taken as a matter of course. They have certainly been generous in their reception of us as their guests at their anniversary of freedom.

'Good winds and Godspeed,' you wished us before we left, our dear friends. Thank you from my young crew. They have experienced a time that comes only once in a lifetime. If another such opportunity should arise, we would love to return.

Again Bjørn is waiting for us. He is there with, generally, the same people who were waiting for us on our trip in. Svein Hurum, who owns the shipping firm Hurum Marine, takes the stern hawser. He has been our agent, without any remuneration. Our friends are asked on board for a meal with us. The boys have a quiet evening at the Seamen's Church. They write home and read newspapers.

The *Christian Radich* is made ready for the trip home. The lifeboats are brought back on board. The much-despised chemical toilets, which are not supposed to smell but which stink like hell, are sent quickly ashore, and our own are installed again. The ship's belly is filled with fuel, fresh water, and provisions for four to five weeks.

On the last evening Bjørn invites the whole adult crew for a farewell dinner on shore. Marvelous food, good music, and beautiful, topless dancers. We have a final good night drink and go on board early. Our reporter friend, Paul Galloway, has been active since he left us in Chicago: all of the formalities I warned him about, in case he wanted to sign on and sail with us to Europe, have not scared him off. He has contacted Østlandets Skoleskib and been given the go-ahead signal, has gotten his medical certificate, has been given leave from his job, and has said goodbye to his friends and acquaintances.

Paul Galloway adjusts completely to the atmosphere on board. He knows us from before and, in addition, like so many others, has fallen in love with the ship, and he is fascinated by the fact that we sail her with sixteen-year-olds.

He is determined to like fishballs, which he has heard is a Norwegian specialty. Almost none of the officers like fishballs.

He has never been on saltwater before.

Late in the morning, on September 8, we set sail. The celebration of the bicentennial and the official visits have come to an end. Now we put to sea. A new chapter has begun. For me, personally, too. I was forty-six years old yesterday.

This afternoon and tomorrow we are to give written exams to the boys. Instruction has been irregular on a trip such as the one we have made, and it is a long time since we began their instruction, in the Trade Winds region. Undoubtedly some of it has been forgotten, but we'll have to let them show what they remember. Of course, it isn't just this theoretical knowledge that counts. They have become practitioners, too. Ship maintenance, turns at the helm, lookout, engine-room watch – they have learned all of the routine.

They have also learned a good deal that cannot be measured in grades or numbers. They have learned something about themselves. Maybe they don't notice this, themselves, but those around them do. This is where a sailing ship has its strength. Just pure object lessons. In teamwork, learning to rely on themselves, to depend on their comrades, to live together, and to work together.

Even the very slowest understand that if everyone doesn't haul on the rope at the same time nothing happens. Cooperation is necessary. They have also learned a little bit about how people in a few other countries live and think. These are valuable lessons to learn. They have experienced a summer full of impressions, which will take a long time to sort out.

We have been privileged, we who were given the chance to sail the *Christian Radich* this summer.

At 1025 hours on September 9, the pilot disembarks at Les Escoumains, the mouth of the Saint Lawrence River and the last pilot station on the way out. This afternoon we finished with the exams for the cadets, and now it is normal sea watches.

Before 'time off' (in other words, at the end of the day's work), we muster at the lifeboats. It has been a long time since we last did this. We have tried to make it a part of the regular exercises, but the nature of our trip has made this impossible. The alarm sounds, and they find their stations. Don life vests! The mates and the senior crew check to see that everyone is in the right spot and knows his duties.

I make the rounds to check that the ship is being made ready for sea. On the fo'c'sle head the starboard anchor is still cockbilled, ready for use. It will hang there until we leave Saint Johns. We are to put in there to replenish.

These huge stock anchors are clumsy to handle. At sea they are brought

The parrel, a device for hauling up and lowering the upper topsail yard when the sail is furled. The track on which the parrel runs is seen as a dark line on the mast.

Practice in wire splicing is a part of the curriculum in learning seamanship.

PHOTOGRAPHS: FINN BERGAN

inboard with the aid of the cat tackle and secured with chains that are 'tightened' with wooden wedges. They are good anchors, which hold under practically any weather conditions, but it is a heavy and old-fashioned system.

This is the way it was on sailing ships.

The mooring cables are nicely coiled up forward of the foremast. The base is the pinrail around the mast foot. Yup, she looks shipshape. The new deck the men laid in Hommelvik doesn't appear to have been damaged at all by the 200,000 to 300,000 people who tramped on board her this summer.

On the boat deck the two forward lifeboats are secured in their chocks. The lifeboat maneuver is finished, and the life vests are put back in place in the lockers between the boats.

The fan in the galley skylight on the boat deck hums softly and carries with it unmistakable smells of preparations for supper. The galley trainees are undoubtedly in the process of preparing the day's or, more correctly, the night's bread baking. They are at an age when they really pack it away, these boys, and manage to down thirty to forty loaves every day.

The main deck looks fine. All the ropes are coiled as they should be, with the bottom edge of the coil one foot from the deck. The large, homemade fenders are lashed under the quarterdeck ladder, as are a couple of extra oil drums. I am glad we changed the wooden door leading from the main deck, last winter. Now we have a good, watertight aluminum door, which can withstand the blows when she ships water.

Can't be helped that it was done at the cost of nostalgia!

On the quarterdeck things are as they should be. Shipshape. The hawsers at the stern are coiled behind the rudder trunk. When we leave Saint Johns, we will pass them (which means haul them) forward to the sail locker to get them out of the way. The tackle for the lifeboats has been tightened, with extra lashings around, to prevent the boats from shifting in high seas.

In the charthouse we have a piece of equipment that the old boys from the time of sailing ships would not have understood. Advanced equipment, for which my electronics training from twenty-five years ago is not enough. The first mate is in charge of the electronics. He has a feeling for this, is more or less self-taught, and usually gets everything working correctly.

The radar hums along. This is a must in today's dense traffic. The watch receiver is switched onto the emergency frequency, 2182 kH, and the radio-telephone, the VHF, is on channel 16, the emergency channel. The weather chart recorder is mounted on the after bulkhead of the radio room. It gives us printed weather charts covering large areas of ocean. This is very reassuring.

The Decca is mounted on the port side of the charthouse. This is switched on to the Canadian chain that covers our waters for the time being. Its red, green, and violet dials indicate hyperbolic position lines and give cross bearings directly on the Decca chart. Electronics has made life easier for the navigator. Today's shipping industry demands more and more automation in all sectors. Instruments are taking over for the seaman. But just let us be on our guard about all of this. Let's not allow ourselves to become the slaves of technology to the extent that, if the instruments and the computers give up the ghost, we have forgotten our elementary knowledge as seamen.

Forward in the sail locker there is the good smell of rope and sails. We still have some of the old hempen sails in reserve. They are heavy and unwieldy compared to the new dacron sails we got last year. On the after bulkhead and along the racks, blocks of all sizes are hanging. He keeps things in order, does the boatswain.

Aft of the cadets' bathroom are the two mess decks that are the boys' 'home.' Here is where they sleep, they eat, and this is where they are given their instruction. You could call the furnishings rather spartan, with benches and chests lined up fore and aft, tables bolted to the deck, and hooks for the hammocks fastened to the deck above.

PHOTOGRAPH: STIG NÆSS

Primitive but functional. We would have preferred an arrangement with fixed bunks, but it is expensive to remodel a ship. Money has always been a problem for us.

In the passageway aft of the mess decks the new twelve-cylinder GM engine throbs. It is always a relief when the ship is under sail and the 'churn' can be shut off.

The crew mess was given a real facelift in Hommelvik. Materials were sent as a gift for both the mess and the saloon from the firm Hovde A/S in Trondheim. The crew repaneled the mess during the course of a weekend, on their own time.

Further aft, on the port, is a room that previously was used as a workshop. To replace this we now have a very good cadets' workshop on deck, in an extended galley deckhouse.

If we are to follow up the new training plans, we have to have space for a couple of extra instructors, and, because of this, this room will, in time, be remodeled into two cabins. Way aft, under the saloon, is the depot. The ship's sergeant rules here with an iron hand. Uniforms, pea jackets, extra caps, foul-weather gear, and long underwear borrowed from the navy are stacked neatly on the shelves. Order is a virtue, particularly at sea.

I have a cup of coffee in the charthouse. The coffee pot has a habit of tipping over in high seas. Last year it spilled all over the chart. We then swore that a special shelf would be made for the pot. But the pot is still standing on the chart table.

Far out in the bay some pure white whales are playing. According to the pilots we had outbound, there is a 'family' staying here all year round. I have counted ten of them that come up and blow at regular intervals. Fortunately, they are protected.

We follow the marked route out and report to the Coast Guard at every control point. It is the American Coast Guard with whom we have been in contact, in particular, and not only on the lakes. Throughout the whole trip, we have had the feeling that they have taken special care of the *Christian Radich*. Our great Lady of a square-rigger has roused enormous interest, and she deserves it that people hold the door open for her. And they certainly have!

It is Sunday, September 12. Exactly one year ago we started out from New York, bound for Hommelvik. Today we are to call on Saint Johns. The pilot embarks in the afternoon. He takes us in between the high mountains that encircle the harbor. I have called the consul, to arrange for a berth. We are placed ahead of a Portuguese trawler. On the pier there are hundreds of oil drums. Some of them have begun to leak, and this juice from the innermost parts of the earth has been mixed with sand and mud to form a sticky, black mass. I don't want this mess on the new decks. Old polishing rags and painting tarpaulins are sacrificed as doormats.

The consul and the agent come on board. Mail that has been forwarded is dealt out. The agent has an easy job. We want only water and fuel. And some fresh vegetables. He promises to deliver everything on board tomorrow morning.

Thousands of Norwegian fishermen know this port. Saint Johns. The bay is protected from all winds, with the exception of the easterlies.

It is obvious that all activity in this place is geared to fishing and shipping. Bunker stations, a small shipyard with a slipway, fish processers, ships' chandlers. All of this can be found here. It must have been a very lively place in the days when the famous Bank schooners based their activity here. Ships like the *Gazela Primeiro,* which was subjected to such rough treatment during the 'battle of Bermuda' have undoubtedly put in here many, many times during their long fishing careers.

I stroll ashore in the evening to stretch my legs. The city isn't exactly what you would call swinging. Sunday is evidently not the day people amuse themselves in Saint Johns. Doesn't really matter. A pub serves good beer. A cozy place, spoiled, though, with a jukebox, 'canned music.'

I walk a bit along quiet streets and then go on board. There she lies, our ship. Ahead of the trawler, which could stand a little maintenance.

The watch reports all hands aboard. Good. Tomorrow we'll be busy before we set out to sea. If the weather is good, we'll stop on the Banks to fish. Newly purchased fishing gear is just waiting to be tried out. We have plans for a prize for the largest fish.

The boys have asked if we'll have rough weather on the trip, if they'll get to see anything besides a calm sea, which is all there has been on the trip so far. They, after all, are going to be sailors. OK, boys. Maybe you'll have a chance to see that the ocean has many faces. There'll be plenty of time for you to see a rough sea.

I open the cabin porthole before I hit the sack. In comes a smell of oil, fish, and dirty harbor water. The water ripples and gurgles around the dock poles and the lines creak softly – well-known sounds which are safe to go to sleep by.

'Captain, six-thirty.' I am roused by the young voice of one of the mess boys. Soon the familiar sounds of the morning cleaning can be heard. The decks are swabbed down, and I hear the boatswain chewing out somebody or other. A quick shower. A luxury that will not be available, from now on. On the trip across we have to save fresh water. We have 100 tons for 103 men. This must do for making food, necessary washing, and the brushing of teeth. Before breakfast I manage to write a couple of letters, both official and private. This will be the last mailing ashore until Europe.

After morning roll call, it's 'all out,' as the boys say. This means really busy. Bunkering from the tank truck. The carpenter takes charge of filling water. The chief officer and the steward supervise activities. I have to take care of the consul, who has come aboard early in the morning. The agent arrives, too, and bills are to be signed. The agent doesn't have much time and goes ashore.

We invite the consul to lunch. Chicken and fresh salad are nothing to be ashamed of. Afterwards we sit and chat until he has to go. I accompany him to the gangway. 'Good luck, Captain.' 'Thank you, Mr. Consul.'

XII

HOMEWARD BOUND

I go to the charthouse to get the latest weather forecast from the Coast Guard. They answer immediately on the VHF. 'Well, sir, the forecast for the next two days is as follows . . .' Light winds to begin with, but increasing westerly winds later on. Fine. I would like a westerly, force six.

We sail on the thirteenth. This isn't good, but we are in a hurry. The tug swings us around, and the pilot takes us out of the harbor. He disembarks and we unfurl all our canvas in a pretty light wind.

Finally, finally we are homeward bound. 'Make her ready for sea.' The starboard anchor is laid inboard and lashed well. The hawse pipes are plugged with rags to prevent spray getting under the fo'c'sle when she pitches in the sea.

In the saloon the steward is packing everything that can move around in rough seas. He replaces the white tablecloth with a coarsely woven rubberlike cloth, on which the tableware stays steady even in relatively high seas.

Supper at 1800 hours. Sea routine. Throughout the whole summer we have had guests at every meal, aside from the last few days after Montreal. Well, Paul is with us, of course, but he is one of the boys now. From now on the youngsters will have to survive on ship's food. Delicacies from America, where they were spoiled in that way, are a thing of the past. No more daily consumption of hamburgers, steaks, and banana splits.

Sea watches are set. The off watch turns in. Life on board falls into a rhythm that will last until Europe. A good rhythm.

The evening watch lowers the topgallants and royals. They go aloft and furl. We do this almost as routine, when we aren't racing. It is not too pleasant to send men on the top yards if we are surprised by a gale at night.

The sun goes down behind the mountains, which can still be seen in the blue

A pleasant evening on the fo'c'sle.
PHOTOGRAPHS: FINN BERGAN

mist to the west. It is getting chillier. The helmsman strikes seven bells, seven-thirty. We sail eastward toward a dark, fall horizon.

I have been lying on my bunk reading boat brochures. I am collecting ideas for my own boat, which is being built. I've sold the fishing smack *Freyja,* which I've had for twelve years. She was built by a chap in Hardanger, one of these small farmers who used to have boat building as an extra job.

In this business it is hard to keep a boat, much less use it. But when I retire, sometime in the future, I have to have my own craft. It is possible, of course, to survive without one, but what kind of life is that? Once you're bitten by the bug...

Trønderverftet in Hommelvik is building my dream boat. In steel. I can afford the hull. The rest will have to come gradually. At every opportunity I have wandered around in yacht harbors and marinas to study just how boats of the same size are equipped. Cecil Stephansen has designed my boat. He is an experienced designer, with a lot of boats to his record.

Here I am, aboard a square-rigger under sail in the Atlantic, and dreaming about my hobby. Boats and sailing. I'm one of the lucky ones who has his hobby as his job and actually gets paid for it.

Wind, west-southwest, force five to six. Through the open porthole I hear the commands when the watch wears around to run with the wind. The boys are experienced now, so there isn't so much that has to be said. Boys' voices repeat the orders: 'Fast the mainsail, fast the lower topsail, fast the topsail, fast the topgallant, fast the royal.' 'All squared away.' I hear the braces being coiled on the pinrail on the starboard side above the cabin. They work in the dark without any problems. They know how to do this now.

I go up on the quarterdeck. It is my habit at sea to be awake during the night. Surprises are always more difficult to cope with in the dark. Oncoming traffic, wearing around, unexpected gales. But right now it's perfect weather. She rocks along with the sea swishing along the ship's sides. A following sea and slight yawing on the course. The helmsmen have become experienced. They allow her to veer evenly on either side of the course without using the wheel too much. She likes it that way.

It's a fine night. The dark sky is strewn with stars. The high masts draw an uneven sinus curve over the blanket of stars as we ride eastward. It's good to stand at the railing in the dark. Letting your thoughts wander. The railing is made of teak and feels good to the touch. The buoy watch brings me a cup of coffee. Strong coffee, which we drink often. The gleams of light from the after cabins light up the following waves that are breaking with a pleasant sound.

This element first got its hold on me, now when was it? It must have been when I sailed as a young boy as crew on a B-Dragon in Kristiansand. The sea and ships and boats. The dream and interests of a great many Norwegian boys down through the ages. One learns respect for the sea gradually. With experience. Never expose yourself to the blows. If you do, the sea is a kleptomaniac, which collects human lives.

You find great freedom out here. Freedom where you and your ship are independent of land and cities and stress. A freedom where you get the strength from nature to bring your ship to its destination. Your ship is an independent society where one man has the responsibility. Here it is you.

My first command was a submarine. Almost twenty years ago. Now, here I stand, on board a sailing ship. One could call this regression.

In the charthouse it is pleasant, nice and cozy. The chart shows our position as even jumps marked off by each watch. The radar screen doesn't show any echo. With as good weather conditions as we now have, we usually let it stand on the twelve-mile scale.

Second mate Erick Høen shooting the height of the sun. PHOTOGRAPH: FINN BERGAN

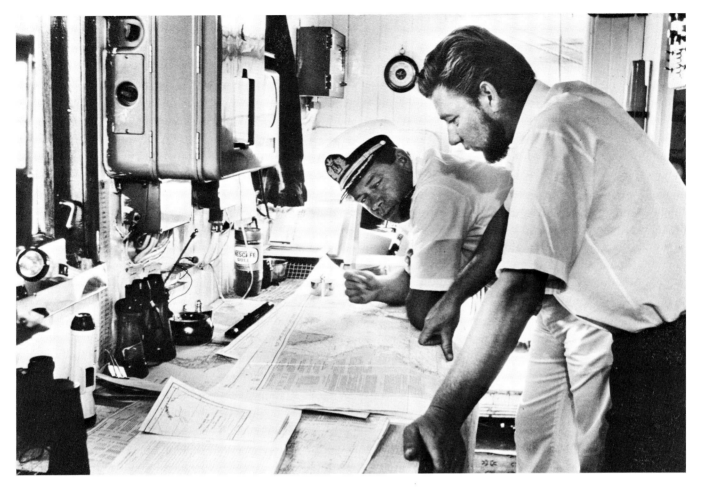

The watch receiver is scraping a little. Atmospheric disturbances on 2182. The VHF is tuned to channel 16. No traffic there.

The captain and the first mate studying the chart.
PHOTOGRAPH: FINN BERGAN

The northerly America route is south of us, so it would mostly be fishing vessels we could meet out here on the Banks. That's right, the Banks. We have to give up our hopes of fishing. The sea is becoming so rough that it is difficult to keep the ship in position, and, besides, we have to use the favorable westerlies.

Last year we were enveloped by fog way at the south end of the Banks. The radar showed that we were more or less surrounded by fishing vessels. Our engine had gone to the Happy Hunting Grounds, so we just lay there and drifted. An echo on the radar approached on a collision course. We called on our radio, but no answer.

Then – out of the fog came a ship with full deck lighting and sharp floodlights. The ship turned to port and passed us at a cable's distance. From strong loudspeakers we suddenly heard odd, Oriental music. Not one man on deck or on the bridge, as far as we could see.

A Japanese factory ship, perhaps. The ship disappeared astern into the thick fog, which suddenly seemed to become colder and clammier.

Fog at sea is the very devil.

The horizon appears in the east at five-thirty. The lanterns are extinguished. I throw myself on my bunk and am roused for breakfast. The mess boys balance platters and trays with professional competence, after months of training.

Paul and I sit and talk afterwards. A lot of things about the *Christian Radich* and our activities and about youth at sea. He still doesn't seem to comprehend that we sail this ship with fifteen- and sixteen-year-olds. I explain to him, too,

PHOTOGRAPH: FINN BERGAN

why we believe that the sailing ship is an excellent instrument in the basic training of young men who want to go to sea. Paul understands and agrees and wonders why the U.S. doesn't have ships like this. I do, too.

He suddenly looks a little restless, does Paul. He suggests that he take a turn on the deck, for some fresh air. I agree with him. It will probably take some time before the seasickness passes.

The chief engineer reports that the propeller shaft is more or less broken. It isn't that bad, but the bolts in the locking segments between the propeller shaft and the intermediate shaft are cracked. The key groove on the propeller shaft is ruined. The stopper for the key has been worn away. What do we do now?

At the moment we have a good wind, but when we get closer to the Channel I want the engine power in reserve. A real repair job is a job for a shipyard. Maybe we'll have to have a new propeller shaft. We'll have to do something temporary, however. We don't have very many tools for this purpose.

So that the propeller shaft doesn't slide astern and lock the helm when we open the coupling, we pull out the two largest bench vises on board. These are placed firmly on the shaft and wedged against the stuffing box aft. The locking segments are opened, and the whole miserable mess uncovered. A plane is used to round off the metal at the key groove, mostly by feel. New locking bolts are made of mild steel. These should be stronger, but we don't have the materials. The locking key and its support on the shaft are ground. Three quarter-inch set screws are made, and the key is bored through and the screws are threaded into the shaft steel. From my duty on a submarine, I remember trials with gluing the top lug on the torpedoes, steel against steel.

The carpenter's mate is given orders to break out our universal glue, Araldit. The key is glued and screwed tight. The locking segments are screwed into place, and the whole thing is to be left for a couple of days before we try it out. I send a report to Norway about the whole affair and say that the engine can only be used at slow speed. The repairs will take two days.

In the afternoon the deck gang continues to make things ready for the sea. A safety net of nylon rope is braided into the lower rigging to about one-and-a-half meters above the bulwarks. This is to prevent anyone from being washed overboard if we ship a lot of water. Lifelines are stretched out over the main deck, and the hatchway from the deck to the mess decks is shut off. We usually shut this when she ships water over the main deck. A couple of sheets are

When you get used to it, a hammock is fine to sleep in. When you're young and tired, though, you can sleep anywhere.
PHOTOGRAPH: ØIVIND BARBO

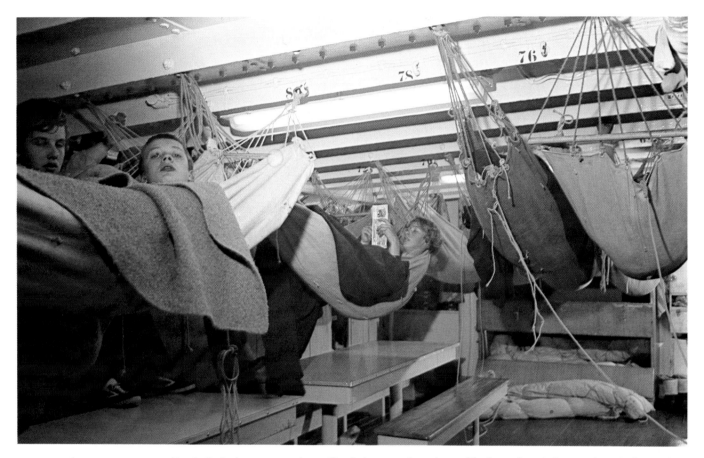

The boys sleep in hammocks, which are slung once the watch is done and everything has been squared away after mealtime.

PHOTOGRAPH: FINN BERGAN

worn, and new ones are spliced. It is important that all of the running rigging is renewed at the first sign of wearing. Ropes are expensive, but safety first.

This work on the rigging is a continuous job. Eighty-five hundred meters of running cordage are to be inspected. About a hundred blocks or more have to be ship hauled. Footropes and backropes are taken down and examined closely once a year, but there is regular inspection of them.

Seizings are replaced as they show wear. Ratlines break, once in awhile, and must be replaced. There's enough to do. This fall we have to inspect the standing rigging. This has to be reserved. A big, time-consuming job. It is a bitter job to work aloft in the wintertime.

Extra servings are put on the lower fore-shrouds to prevent chafing of the foresail. The footropings hit against the shrouds in slight wind. Some of the wire sheets on the foresails have become slightly worn in their servings. The rope is chafed when the sail is hauled over in tacking and with changes in wind direction. We'll just have to let it stay as it is until we get home.

Thus the days pass, in regular routine. Watch follows watch; meals at regular times and the ship's maintenance keep the crew active, as much as the weather permits. In the provisions room food is weighed, the bread machine is in frequent use for our excellent homemade bread. A sixteen-year-old who works hard in fresh air has an enormous appetite. As far as I can remember, the record last year was twenty-one pancakes for breakfast. The person in question obviously liked pancakes. But he did feel 'a little full,' afterwards.

For someone thirty years older, matters are a bit different. The caloric intake must be strictly limited, otherwise the unavoidable result is an addition to already increasing tonnage. I know this from bitter experience.

During the night of Friday, September 17, the main transmitter fails. The first mate works on it for hours, but he finally has to give up. There is current leakage

She likes a fresh wind – here on a port tack. We're doing eight to nine knots.

PHOTOGRAPHS: FINN BERGAN

somewhere or other. We have to give up on getting the box to work until we get hold of a specialist, and that won't be until we reach the other side.

As of September 1, we are a part of the AMVER system. AMVER stands for Automatic Mutual-assistance Vessels Rescue System, and it is run, I almost added 'of course,' by the U.S. Coast Guard. Ships that send reports to AMVER do this as a part of their routine. Once every twenty-four hours they give their position, course, speed, port of arrival, and other information. These data are then fed into a computer, which stores similar data from all reporting ships. Using these data systems, they can maintain a worldwide plot and thus ease any searches, rescues, etc.

Now we have no possibilities for sending regular position reports. We have to report this, and the office in Oslo must be told that they cannot expect to hear from the ship until it is closer to the English coast. Then we will be able to communicate, using our reserve transmitter which normally has a range of 200 nautical miles.

The first mate calls 'all ships' on our reserve transmitter. After a few hours we contact a Danish freighter. Through him we send the message home. We thank the Dane for his aid and wish him bon voyage. We are now alone at sea.

I get out my typewriter. Have to begin on the voyage report. A lot has to be covered to give a fairly clear picture of our eventful summer. I have to try to impart to the reader of the report the fantastic public-relations value this ship has and to do my best to see that this continues to be utilized in the future. I also have to emphasize the value sailing ships have for those young people who are privileged to sail on them. What is good about this privilege is that it is open to everyone. Every Norwegian boy who satisfies the medical requirements can apply for acceptance as a cadet. It has not been easy to convince the school authorities that this is of any particular value in modern times, but I believe this skepticism to be disappearing.

I have to point out the fine impression the youngsters have made on the trip. They are marvelous representatives of our young people and for our country. Naturally, they are not angels. If they hadn't played a few tricks, there would have been something wrong – they wouldn't have been normal.

I mustn't write too much, because then no one wants to read the report. The conclusion must stress the importance of trips like those we have had these last two summers. Norway must bear the expense of keeping this ship and, preferably, put the others under sail, too. We have good spokesmen in both the parliament and the cabinet, so matters appear to be taking a favorable turn. Maybe in time we will find it feasible to build a new ship? The Soviets and the Poles are considering such an idea – in fact, they have actually come further than just considering it. They are on the market to find a shipyard that can take on the job. This is what they have told us, anyhow, and the Poles thought that they had the shipyard capacity for this task.

During the evening of September 21 the wind dies. The weather charts have shown that the dependable westerly has been replaced by very light winds of varying direction. The wind has tossed the compass card around today. Finally we lower and furl the square sails.

Things are now a bit tense. We are to try out our 'home-glued' propeller shaft coupling. If it holds, everything is just fine, but, if the opposite is the case, we are back in the same situation we were in last year. Zero engines, purely a sailing vessel. We don't have time for that this year.

I start up the propeller cautiously. Just a few revolutions to begin with. I let the engine run carefully. In a few hours we'll stop and check the coupling. A thousand revolutions is all I dare give. This is what is needed in quiet seas to

push her forward at about six knots. If she has head winds or currents, she slows down. Then we have to tack all the way, which is time-consuming with a square-rigger, which only sails about sixty to seventy degrees of the wind.

No more peace in the saloon. The engine thumps, and the propeller churns around.

When September 22 is a couple of minutes old, the engine is turned off. The bolts and the coupling are examined. They are okay, and everything looks fine. By gosh, it looks as though the glue is holding. With care, we can perhaps make it to Falmouth.

Even though the new dacron sails are relatively light, many men are needed to furl the mainsail.

XIII

THE HURRICANE

It has been cloudy for several days. Impossible to shoot the height of the sun and/or the stars. The sun has just barely peeked out a couple of times. The mate on watch runs to the charthouse, grabs the sextant, but just as he is about to 'take the sun down on the horizon,' to measure its height, the modest orb disappears behind a cloud.

The latest weather chart shows a couple of smaller low-pressure areas to the west and a small one at the northern end of the Bay of Biscay. The wind tosses again. At lunchtime there is a weak southerly breeze. A few hours later he has gone over to north-northeast. Then a little more northwest. At 5:00 A.M. we wear around to port. The wind increases, and we shorten sails and furl everything except the staysails and the lower topsails.

It gets dark. The navigation lights are switched on at 6:00 A.M. The wind hauls even more northwest. The yards are braced 'square' – downwind. During the last two hours, the wind has increased to wind force nine, strong gale. The sea begins to get rough. By 9:00 P.M. we have a full gale. The staysails are no use. They whip around and pull on the stays. In order to save wear and tear on them, and to save them in time in case this gets worse, we haul them down. I also have to send men out on the jibboom to secure the foresails. Best to do this before the sea gets too rough. The wind is now directly astern, almost from the west. The sea is really rough, and to ease steering we lower the lower mizzen-topsail and furl it carefully. Men are sent aloft to fix the gaskets. These gaskets are ropes tied around yards and sails to reinforce the ordinary seizings. The ventilator cowls on the large ventilator tubes on the main deck, leading down to the inside of the ship, are taken off, and canvas is lashed over the top to prevent their filling when we ship water.

We have goose-winged the lower fore-topsail. This means that only part of the lower fore-topsail is set. PHOTOGRAPH: FINN BERGAN

Paul lives in the ship's office. He has fallen out of his bunk a couple of times. He comes topside to watch the ocean in an uproar – and doesn't really look too happy.

Everyone is turned out and given orders to stand by in foul-weather gear. The watch is kept on deck, while the off watch can flop down on the mess deck when they're not needed. By ten o'clock in the evening the extra seizings have been set on the foreroyal and topgallant. She's tossing violently now. Only senior crew members are sent aloft to fix the gaskets. There is danger that the sails can blow out, and 1½-inch nylon rope is used.

It's dark aloft, in the rigging. I can barely see the men as they fight their way aloft with a coil of rope over their shoulders. Good men. They can be depended on in tight corners.

The barometer is still falling. It's very low. This can mean a lot of things. It's obvious that a powerful low-pressure area is forming or will sweep over us.

But what course and what speed does the center have? We should try to blow away from the center. We have no business being there. I discuss this with the mates. We are about 400 miles from the French coast and are on a course for the Bay of Biscay. We are now doing fourteen knots. I agree with myself to just let her run on this course tonight. If the wind stays in this direction a long time we will have to heave to, but I want to do that by daylight.

2345 hours. The logbook notes that the foreroyal broke out of its seizings.

The wind gauge shows more than sixty knots relative wind. If we add our own speed, we have a well-developed hurricane. Wind forces above sixty-three knots are hurricanes. We can hear hard bangs from the foremast, up there in the dark, drowning out the whistling in the rigging. The mast lights on the crow's nests are lit to ease the work on deck, but aloft it's dark. I can just glimpse the foreroyal where it is flapping wildly. The carpenter, Thorleif Abrahmsen, has been aloft to try to secure the royal, but he has had to give up. The gaskets have parted. One-and-a-half-inch nylon rope is strong, but obviously not strong enough. The

PHOTOGRAPH: TROND O. RØED

The ship rolls in the heavy seas. The lookouts are ordered down from the fo'c'sle, where they ordinarily stand. Here the port lookout is sitting on a lifebelt locker on the quarterdeck.

<small>PHOTOGRAPHS: TORE RØNNIG</small>

buntlines and clewlines break, and the sail is now hanging like a bag on the sheets and the headroping, which is sewed to a round steel bar, the jackstay, on the upper side of the yardarm. The sheets are chains joined to wires that are led in to the mast and from there through blocks and ropes to the deck.

Now the fore-topgallant begins to break out of the gaskets. Men go aloft to secure, but they have to give up. They jump down onto the next yard, the topsail yard, where this sail too has begun to swell out between the seizings. The royal sheets snap. The chain and wires flail the yards below, the stays, and the backstays. The sail is just hanging on the headropings. It flaps with an uncanny sound, which drowns out everything else. Sparks fly where worn wires and chains hit the yards, the backstays, and the stays. The topgallant sheets break. Same thing happens here. The loose sails make the whole foremast sway. The top of the mast sways three to four feet in either direction, and this creates an enormous strain on the stays. The topsail can't be secured, either. Now the forecourse begins to break loose. 'Secure the forecourse, men!' It will really be a crisis if this gives way, too. The huge sail can wind itself around the forestays. If these break, the foremast will come down. Luckily, the men are able to secure the forecourse...

The same miserable process now begins on the mainmast. The royal and the topgallant suffer the same fate as those on the foremast. Both masts sway threateningly, and I expect breakage any moment.

If those damned sails could just flail themselves to pieces!

Dacron is extremely strong. If these had been hempen sails, like those used in

102

Shipping water on the main deck. The pictures have been taken from the foot of the ladder to the fo'c'sle. We are looking at the port railing awash – and the safety net stretched above the bulwarks.

Lower main-topsail about to tear loose. This was the last sail that could be used to keep the ship into the wind.

the old days, they would have blown to bits long since. It would be too bad to lose these sails, which are only one year old. The crew is working hard up there, but, finally, it's no use any longer. Worn-out wires, ends of chains, and ropes flail at the rigging. It's really hazardous working aloft now. Besides, it's blowing so hard that they have more than enough to do, just to hang on. They have done a prodigious job. As I said, you can depend on them in a tight squeeze.

I go forward with First Mate Hegerstrøm. He is also responsible for rig maintenance. 'Do you think the foremast will hold?'

It looks bad. The royal and topgallant backstays are shaking, and the rigging screws are getting warm. This is a sign of material fatigue. There are cracks like gunshots from above. The whole ship is shaking. How long can this go on? The watch is evacuated from the fo'c'sle. If the mast comes down, it can go through the deck.

The cadets are sent to the quarterdeck, where we can keep them under supervision. We brace the topgallant and royal yards on the mainmast as much fore and aft as possible, to put the yards in the wind direction. In this way I hope

Eerie mood at dawn while the ship rushed on like a wounded bird. PHOTOGRAPH: TROND O. RØED

to reduce the violent shaking of the mast. The main-topmast forestay, which supports the lower mast fore and aft, begins to give way. A couple of the strands in the double stay, made of 3½-inch wire, have snapped.

What do we do if the masts come down? How can we cut the heavy shroud wires? Our portable gas-cutting equipment is undoubtedly useless with all the water we're shipping. The worst thing would be if the yards and mast ends go overboard and still hang on the stays. They might knock holes in the side of the ship. I don't like the situation at all. It is very bad.

The barometer is still falling, although not as rapidly. Paul has been hanging on, knocking at the glass for several hours, in the hope that it would rise. This will make copy for you to write home about, Paul.

The sea runs even higher. She looks like a wounded bird, our ship, as she races along. It is not a pretty sight, aloft. Fortunately, the sails begin to rip to pieces. The loose chain and wire ends beat holes in the canvas, but it takes time before they tear. The starboard side of the mainsail begins to blow out of the seizings. The ship's sergeant, Sigvart Johanssen, goes aloft to 'lock' the sail, so that it can't keep on loosening along the yard. The sheet snaps. He can't manage to catch hold of the canvas.

The main tack, a three-inch rope that is fastened to the clew along with the sheet, is still intact. This rope is passed astern, up on the quarterdeck. Here the cadets give all they've got, and the sail is hauled in to the mast and lashed around this and the lower rigging. The great strain placed on the lower rigging when the yard whipped wildly back and forth has stopped. An unorthodox way of furling the mainsail, but it works.

The sails left are unevenly distributed on the masts. The foremast is left with a furled forecourse. The lower topsail has been whipped to pieces by the sails that broke out earlier, which now hang in rags. The mainmast looks a little better. Here we have secured the topsail. The lower topsail is still intact. The

Some of the waves swept all the way up to the bridge. PHOTOGRAPH: OLAV SKOGEN

mizzenmast is the best of all. No losses here. The sails on this mast were furled earlier and have been easier to keep an eye on from the quarterdeck.

Our Lady is now racing across the storm-beaten sea with one lower topsail set. The sea has roughened up to about fortyfoot waves. The ship is still doing fourteen knots.

Day breaks. The eastern sky pales about five o'clock, and an hour later I want to heave to. We cannot keep on toward land indefinitely at this speed. Now it's light enough to be able to work on deck without artificial lighting. I want to use the engine to bring her around. We could do it with only the lower main-topsail, but propeller water on the rudder is a big help in bringing her around quickly.

I study the waves that froth astern. There are three or four waves that look a little 'kinder' than most of them do. 'Hard astarboard. Pull hard on port braces. (This means to close haul her on the starboard tack.) Check the braces and don't let the lower main-topsail fill too much.'

Flat out on engine. How is that coupling doing? I have decided to use full speed ahead only in an emergency. Which is now. She has to come around before she takes the breakers with the wind and sea abeam.

We do it. We steady her fifty to sixty degrees off the wind. The yards on the mizzenmast are braced round in such a way that they lie perpendicular to the wind. The wind caught in these sails helps to keep the stern down and thereby bring the bow into the wind. We secure a small piece of canvas on the weather side of the lower mizzen-shrouds, just enough to give steerageway.

Here we lie, hove to. She takes the waves elegantly but heels violently. The wind is still blowing a good wind force twelve. At times she ships water sharply. The engine is set at slow speed, just enough to help in steering. The lower main-topsail begins to burst her seams. The canvas has loosened in the clews.

I go down to my cabin to get a package of cigarettes. I do a lot of smoking

Decks swabbed, free of charge.
PHOTOGRAPHS: TORE RØNNIG

now. What a mess there is in here! There's a leak from the deck somewhere. Everything is wet – bunk, couch, books, and clothes. Maybe it comes from the charthouse just above, where water gurgles on the deck.

In the passageway outside the saloon, it is also wet. Water leaks from the deck, through the new redwood panels. Behind these there are electric cables. This can't be doing them any good. Somebody among the galley personnel has managed to make coffee and fried eggs. I sit down on the deck in the charthouse with my plate on my lap.

The motor launch breaks loose. A man rushes down to the sail locker and fetches a few fathoms of strong rope. Straps are fastened around the boat and tightened. They work fast, the crew, but everyone is worn out. Two of the sails on the jibboom break out. Second Mate Erik Høen takes two youngsters with him and crawls out to furl the sails. I don't like it. Pieces of wire are flailing wildly around out there.

Everything goes well.

The cadets are summoned to the mess decks. I talk to them and explain the situation. They have been fantastic tonight, these young kids. I haven't noticed any signs of nervousness. They have worked on the main deck while we shipped water. They are wet and freezing and exhausted, but in great spirits.

They are very interested in knowing if we have made contact with land. 'As I said, we are too far from shore to make direct radio contact, boys, but later we'll try to make contact through another vessel. At the moment we are hove to, until conditions improve.'

Conditions are not going to improve in the immediate future, it appears. Throughout the morning the rigging takes more punishment. It holds, but it is obvious that the stays are slackening and that the masts are tossing even more.

Oddly enough, most of the antennas appear to be intact, at least the output effect on the reserve transmitter is registering. The first mate calls on 2182, hoping that a ship will answer. We should have a good chance of being heard in these waters, with the heavy traffic.

I have drafted a message to inform those at home of the situation. This must be done as temperately as possible, in order not to cause anxiety among the many parents who have their sons on board. I am aware that this will be made much of in the news media. On the other hand, I can't wait too long. The antennas will disappear if the rigging goes. Then we would be left with just the emergency radio aerials for the lifeboats, and they are not much use in this weather.

Nope, I'll have to report that we are lying here with inadequate sails and are waiting for the weather to improve. If it doesn't get better and if the ship continues to take a beating, then I will have to decide if it's necessary to call for assistance.

'All ships, all ships, this is the Norwegian Sail-Training Ship *Christian Radich*. Do you hear me? Over.'

1330 hours. Received report that a French weather-forecasting ship is headed toward us. Constant contact with the Cape Brøvig. *A British freighter is searching for us.*

The first mate's calls are answered, after awhile, by a Norwegian ship, the *Cape Brøvig*. We ask the ship to send a message on our position and our situation to the closest coastal radio station. *Cape Brøvig* sends our message to Lands End radio in England. They act quickly and broadcast the message to all ships nearby. Gradually a lot of vessels report in and offer their help.

What I am mainly interested in is an accurate position, so that I know just how far we can drift without running into rocks. For the time being we certainly have enough room, but if the weather continues like this for a couple of days or

Remnants of the fore-topsail left hanging on the leech. Dacron is strong, and it took hours before the sails blew out.

so, what then? I calculate that we are drifting at about three or four knots, in an easterly direction.

The mate on watch writes in the log: a Dutch tugboat has heard our messages and offers assistance. No cure, no pay. They want a fast answer. This begins to smell strongly of a rescue action, and that was not the idea.

I receive the latest weather report from Lands End via the *Cape Brovig*, but it is far from promising. No changes in the next twelve hours. However, in the meantime, the barometer has risen a little. It feels as though the wind is dropping, also. Hard squalls are still being registered on the wind gauge, but it is quiet in between the gusts of wind.

Late in the afternoon we make contact with the French weather ship, the *France I*. 'Thanks for your assistance' to the *Cape Brovig* and the English freighter. Helpfulness is widespread at sea.

1500 hours. Hove the ship to on the port tack. Drifted northeastward, rough seas, main deck awash.

It is not quite in accord with the facts that we 'hove to' on the other course. We were 'heaved to.' Which means that the ship was thrown round by the boiling seas. It doesn't make any difference, really. We brace round and let her lie like this.

1730 hours: Lit lanterns and deck lights.

We can hear the Frenchman approaching. Our radio contact gets stronger. At 1930 hours he finds us. Radar is a good gadget to have. We are given an exact position, 47° 17' N, 14° 25' W. The position is immediately noted on the chart. Our 'dead reckoning' position isn't bad at all, thirty miles off. It could have been worse.

At 2000 hours a French frigate comes up on lee side. I welcome both vessels. We have contact on our portable VHF set. The main VHF set has been ruined by the saltwater that has forced its way in along the antenna cable.

107

PHOTOGRAPH: TROND O. RØED

Remnants of a topsail. The wind tied the most peculiar 'knots and hitches' with the loose ends.

This is how the hurricane played havoc with sails and running rigging. The picture was taken from the quarterdeck (the bridge) and shows the remnants of the sails, which blew out, on the foremast and mainmast. We are headed into the wind with the engine at slow speed.

Lands End radio is informed that we have been located and that the French vessels will remain by us as long as we wish. The only thing we need is a vessel to act as a communications relay station.

During the night I have sent reassuring reports home that everything is under control and that the crew is fine. It is a comfort to know that the relatives need have no cause for anxiety. I tell the French frigate commander that we need communications aid only. However, he has been given orders to stay with us for the time being. The weather ship is in no hurry, either, and both of them remain in the vicinity until the following morning.

I have spent a couple of hours on a bench in the saloon. The mess boy has carried out everything that is wet in my cabin. They have dried up the water on the deck in the chartroom. There no longer is any leakage into my cabin, and it will gradually become livable again.

24/9–76 (September 24, 1976).
0405 hours: Close-hauled on port tack.
0415 hours: Set main- and mizzen-topmast staysails. Began to steer towards the English Channel.

The wind has dropped considerably, and the sea has calmed down little by little. The wind is blowing from the southeast now, and we are creeping in towards the Channel. At six o'clock we extinguish our lanterns and send men aloft to cut down the worst of the remnants of the sails and the ruined running rigging.

Late in the morning, September 23. The rigging doesn't look very pretty. The helmsmen struggle to keep the ship on course.

0900 hours: Notified the two French ships that further assistance was unnecessary. Sent message via the French frigate to Lands End radio that we would not be heard from until we were within the emergency radio's range (200 nautical miles).

'Thanks for your assistance, men; bon voyage.'

1410 hours: Stopped engines and checked lubrication level and shaft coupling.

The glue is still working. Then we can hope that the shaft is usable until we get to Falmouth. I take a chance and increase to 1,200 revolutions on the engine. Wonder if we should take out a patent for gluing propeller shafts.

The staysails are examined. Just as we thought, two of them have begun to rip at the seams. They have to be patched. The sails are hauled down and brought down to the mess deck, which is acting as sail loft. Bring out the sewing machine. Our versatile first mate is the sailmaker.

26/9–76
Last night we entered the Decca coverage from the Irish chain. We have an

111

The boys try to get a little rest on the mess deck in the high seas.   PHOTOGRAPHS: TROND O. RØED

accurate position at any given time. This is a relief. The tidal currents are getting stronger as we approach the Channel. We have inadequate sails, a propeller shaft that I cannot quite depend on.
The Christian Radich *is motor-sailing with engine and staysails only. We expect to make landfall at the Scilly Isles, off Lands End, later in the day.*

Good old England. It will be good to see you again!

Opposite page: Working in the rigging after the hurricane has wreaked its havoc. We can see a few rags left of the blown-out sails. Eight sails were destroyed.

Boys in the rigging. Aloft on the mizzen-top-gallant and the royal. PHOTOGRAPHS: FINN BERGAN

Monday, September 27, 1976. Underway from St. Johns to Falmouth. 0225 hours: Anchored in Falmouth Harbor, three shackles in the water. Pilot disembarked.

THANKS FOR OUR SUMMER TOGETHER, BOYS!

'Finished at the helm, finished with engines.'

The great wheel is turned until the indicator points midships. The noisy GM engine is stopped. The mate on watch picks out bearing objects and plots anchor bearings on the chart. The cadet on watch on the quarterdeck is to check the position at regular intervals.

I am worn out. The harbor is quiet, and, in the many windows over on the shore, lights shine peacefully. I stand at the railing and look in towards the city.

It is three o'clock. In the morning. I must go and lie down a couple of hours. The tug will take us alongside the dock at seven o'clock. We are to go to Scilley Cox & Co. That's where we had the bottom painted before the race. That seems a long time ago.

This is a harbor rich in tradition. An unknown number of Norwegian sailing ships have put in right here. 'Falmouth for order' was a familiar idea for skippers in the old days. Scilley Cox & Co. have specialized in docking and repairs and today recommend 'Falmouth for repairs.' That is just fine with us at this moment. That good old windjammer the *Christian Radich* has taken a beating, and a really hard one. She looks weary. Rags of sails are still hanging in the rigging. We must cut down the mess in the morning.

It's an odd feeling to lie down on my bunk and know that we are in contact with land on our side of the Atlantic. Even though this contact is through an anchor chain to the 'drag' lying buried in the mud of Falmouth Harbour.

It is difficult to sleep, to relax – an anticlimax. My pleasure in having arrived

Innumerable young men have furled the mainsail down through the years.

with all men in good condition runs out in a sort of lethargy, all the way into my marrow. We have fought against the Atlantic and have come out of the battle with our skins fairly whole, all of us. One hundred and three men.

My thoughts race. Can only think in short sentences, really. My throat is dry from too many cigarettes, coffee, and lack of sleep.

I hope that all of the boys' relatives know that all is well with their young sons. They have reason to be proud of them. I am.

I suppose I should thank the powers that be that everything went well. I do, too, in my own way.

On September 22 we entered this storm. On September 22, nineteen years ago, the German school- and-freight ship, the four-masted bark *Pamir* went down off the Azores, during a hurricane.

The machine-ship personnel of Scilley Cox & Co. take care of the propeller coupling. They shake their heads when they see how we have 'repaired' the damage. The glue gave up, incidentally, just as we arrived at Falmouth.

Our electronic equipment is given a thorough overhaul. After a couple of days, everything is ready. Veritas' representative has approved the temporary repairs of the damages we have registered. The damages list has been sent to our insurance company, and reports have been mailed to the office in Oslo. The reserve sail is bent as far up as the topsail. We are ready to sail home.

Paul says goodbye to us. He has to report home to Chicago as soon as possible. It is a quiet farewell, with a man we have learned to treasure, a man who had his great dream of sailing with a square-rigger across the Atlantic fulfilled.

On October 5 we enter Oslo Fjord. Cold autumn rains gleam on the rocks there at the high-water mark. Nature is already in the process of losing her autumn glory. Boats meet us at Nesoddtangen. They escort us into the harbor basin on this cold, rainy afternoon.

A couple of thousand people are standing and waiting on the pier. I see my wife with her huge umbrella, which was a gift from Toledo. Gangway ashore. Forming ranks and welcoming speeches from the chairman of the board and a few others. Flowers. The boys are allowed to go ashore and greet their relatives, who are waiting. It isn't only raindrops that run down their cheeks.

There they go, running ashore, these boys of mine. We have had six eventful months together. You have represented our country over there in America in a manner you can be proud of. That you have learned something during this time we know. Perhaps about yourselves, mainly, but about other people, too, about your comrades on board and about people you met ashore, underway.

I hope that this summer has given you something that will be valuable ballast throughout the rest of your lives.

Thank you for our summer together, boys. Good luck!

A satisfied skipper.   Photograph Olav Skogen

'Rasmus' (the nickname for the sea) sends hearty greetings on board. PHOTOGRAPH FINN BERGAN

Wherever we sail, we are escorted by pleasure craft. PHOTOGRAPH: NTB

POSTSCRIPT

In this book I have tried to point out the value of a sailing ship for the basic training of future seamen. It can perhaps be called recruit training.

Of course, a knowledge of sails and other 'old-fashioned' matters has no relevance in our modern computer age. But the sailing ships and the modern superships have one thing in common: the sea, the element in which they both operate. A knowledge of and a respect for the sea is what one gains fully on a sailing ship, which depends on weather and winds in a completely different manner than a modern ship does.

The youngsters learn that cooperation and solidarity make them strong. The rigging of a sailing ship is an excellent tool in learning this. It is obvious that everyone must haul on the same rope at the same time to achieve the desired result. Aloft, they learn to rely on themselves and their own strength. They must also have confidence in their comrades in the various working operations that must be carried out to get the ship to sail.

The *Christian Radich* belongs to an institution named Østlandets Skoleskib. She is thus 'privately' owned and is considered in this light to be a private school.

Throughout the years she has sailed in changing economic winds. At times things have been hard, and it has been necessary to go to pure 'rescue actions' a couple of times to save the ship from being laid up and sold.

The response to these actions has shown the ordinary man's willingness and desire to preserve the ship and what she represents. We have an obligation to take care of the bonds binding us to an age in which the country established itself as a shipping nation. We have been much better about preserving our old storehouses and millhouses, in this country, than about protecting the cultural heritage our shipping has brought to us.

The *Christian Radich* is not an old ship and should not be considered a museum. However, she does represent a 'bridge' between the old days and modern times. A bridge on which we take the best in our maritime traditions and try to let the youngsters take them on as ballast on their journey through life. Insofar as is known at the present time, our other two sailing ships, the *Statsråd Lehmkuhl* and the *Sørlandet* are on their way back again as training ships, although in another role than that played by *Christian Radich*.

Our government has, in principle, said that it is willing to help in financing all of the ships.

During the last two years, the *Christian Radich* has been financed practically one hundred percent by the State. The Ministry of Education and Ecclesiastical Affairs has taken care of more than half the costs, and the Ministry of Commerce and Shipping has taken care of the rest. This has covered the purely operational expenditures. Renewing and replacing materials, etc., is partially covered by gifts and partly by funds from the organization Friends of the Christian Radich.

As of 1978, the ship is included in the fiscal budget in the ordinary manner, so that all extra allocations necessary to our survival can be assured, and the tension that waiting for these implies, can be avoided.

In conclusion, I would like to emphasize the public-relations value inherent in sending the ship on trips as a representative. In 1975 and 1976 she was in the U.S.A., and the result was magnificent publicity for Norway. We knew this would happen. The ship had been there before, the last time in 1964, with similar results. A sailing ship captures the imagination of people who have anything at all to do with the sea – and the interest of landlubbers, too. People by the tens of thousands swarm to see these queens of the sea, wherever they appear.

Let us hope that circumstances can be such for our ship, and for the others, too, that they will be refurbished to sail many a salty mile in the future.

View from the mainmast. The two fore lifeboats are passed in toward the midship line. This is done while under sail to spare the mainsail's foot-roping, which, when the ship is close-hauled, will chafe against the boats.

PHOTOGRAPH: FINN BERGAN

PHOTOGRAPH: TROND O. RØED

The old and the new meet. The 'Christian Radich' near 'Ekofisk Charlie', in the North Sea, in 1975.
PHOTOGRAPH: FINN BERGAN

Not everyone knows that the *Christian Radich* was built as a school ship right from the beginning and that she is only forty years old. In other words, the vessel is no leftover from the days of sailing ships in Norway. Even so, the *Christian Radich* has had a checkered career – she has been taken as a prize ship, she has been sunk, and she has beaten forward in financially muddy waters.

The school ship was named for a businessman from Christiania (the former name of Oslo), Christian Radich, who, in 1895, left a sum of money in his will for the building of a new training ship. The condition was that the ship should bear his name. It was not until January 14, 1935, that the institution Oslo Skoleskib decided to build a new vessel. The new school ship would replace the old brig, the *Statsråd Eriksen*, which had been Oslo's training ship since 1901.

A planning committee was appointed, consisting of Commander Kielland, Supervisor Samuelsen, and the captain of the *Statsråd Eriksen*, N. Fredriksen. The director of the Main Naval Shipyard, Captain Chr. Blom, was hired as technical advisor. It was Blom who designed a proposal for the new school ship, according to the requirements set forth, and on the basis of this proposal bids were accepted.

Framnes mekaniske Verksted in Sandefjord submitted the most reasonable

HISTORY
OF THE SHIP

bid, Nkr 595,000, of which Nkr 35,000 was for equipment, and it was decided to have the ship built in Sandefjord. The Norwegian Shipowners' Association helped out with the financing.

The *Christian Radich,* a three-masted square-rigger of 676 gross tons, was constructed in steel with a length of 62.0 meters (204.0 feet), a beam of 9.7 meters (32.0 feet), a molded depth of 5.7 meters (18.0 feet), a draft of 4.5 meters (15.5 feet) and a mast height of 39.0 meters (128.0 feet). She carries twenty-seven sails with a total surface area of 1.350 square meters.

Her keel was laid in August, 1936, and the ship was launched early the following spring. The change-of-ownership trip was made on June 15, 1937.

The old brig, the *Statsråd Eriksen,* which was built as long ago as 1858, was sold to Porsgrunn Skoleskib and continued to sail until the outbreak of the Second World War.

When the war came to Norway in April, 1940, the *Christian Radich* was lying in Horten as a depot ship for the navy. And there she stayed, because the Germans continued to rent her for the same purpose.

But after a time the ship was condemned as a prize and towed to Germany, where she was to do service as a training ship. However, it was difficult to obtain qualified crew members, and, as the war gradually began to be more difficult for Germany, the ship lay there, unused. During docking at Flensburg in January, 1945, the dock was bombed, and the ship sank in fourteen meters (about forty-

Light breeze and sparkling seas...

eight feet) of water. Divers cut her rigging, and somewhat later the wreck was raised.

The war ended, and in 1946 the *Christian Radich* was towed back to Norway to be repaired. The repairs were carried out at the same shipyard that had built her, Framnes, in Sandefjord.

On May 5, 1946, she was again in commission, and now a busy period began aboard the *Christian Radich,* with the training of crews for the merchant fleet, which was to be built up again after the losses during the war.

The *Christian Radich* is operated by an institution that today is called Østlandets Skoleskib. This was founded in 1881, and the founders were cabinet minister C. Jensen, shipowner Plade Stranger, shipyard owner Chr. Brinch, harbor master Chr. J. Johansen, and shipowner R. A. Olsen. The institution's first school ship was called the *Christiania,* and the first cadets came on board on June 7, 1881. The *Christiania* has an obscure past – she was evidently an old East Indiaman, formerly called the *Lady Grey.* In 1901 the *Christiania* was replaced by the *Statsråd Eriksen,* measuring 119 gross tons, and purchased from the navy for Nkr 5,000. The Statsråd was used as a sailing school ship during the summer-half of the year, and the trips were made mainly in North Sea waters. Even before the First World War there was talk of replacing the *Statsråd Eriksen,* and the institution bought a square-rigger, the *Transatlantic,* which could also carry cargo. But the price of ships rose enormously during the war, and in 1917 it was

Above:
Minister of Law of the Sea Questions Jens Evensen (left), Deputy-chairman of Friends of the 'Christian Radich' Harald Tusberg, and Captain Kjell Thorsen before departure from Stavanger, July 4, 1975. The minister was among the crew members on the trip to the U.S.A.

Above, left:
Captain Kjell Thorsen (left), Lasse Kolstad, and Harald Tusberg at the gift presentation ceremony in Oslo, January 27, 1977.

Left:
Managing director Willem Eckhoff (left), of Norsk Texaco Oil, presenting the gift of a check for Nkr 25,000 and a painting of the 'Christian Radich' to the chairman of the school ship's Friends organi-zation, Lasse Kolstad. The painting was done by James E. Mitchell.

Small boy and large wheel.
PHOTOGRAPH: HARALD TUSBERG

The Christian Radichs other 'figurehead', Liv Ullmann.
PHOTOGRAPH: FINN BERGAN

Many are the parents who, during the course of these years, have waved farewell to their beloved sons. Here are former prime minister Trygve Bratteli and his wife Randi.
PHOTOGRAPH: HARALD TUSBERG

decided to sell the *Transatlantic* for a sum of Nkr 800,000. The money was put in the bank while the discussion about building a new ship went on. However, during the depression following the war, the institution lost most of its money, and so the old *Statsråd* continued to sail until she was replaced by the *Christian Radich*.

Operation of the institution Østlandets Skoleskib down through the years has been an endless saga of the battle to make ends meet. Matters have shifted between private operations in the form of gifts, school fees, government subsidies, and other combinations of financing. Today the State, through the ministries of education and commerce and shipping, allocates a sum that just about covers the operating costs. In the future it appears that the ship will come under the auspices of the ministry of education and ecclesiastical affairs only.

It has been a battle for many people who believe in this offer to young people to save the ship. But I hope and believe that the difficult times are now past, and that the *Christian Radich* will sail on for many, many years in a favorable economic breeze.

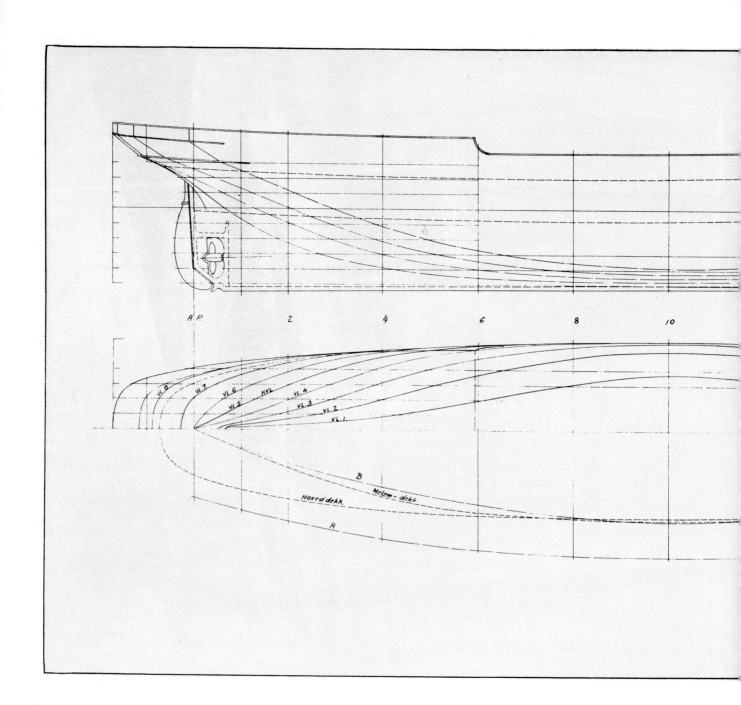

A.P.   2   4   6   8   10

VL.8 VL.7 VL.6 KVL VL.4 VL.3 VL.2 VL.1 VL.5

B   Melem - dekk

Hoved dekk.

H

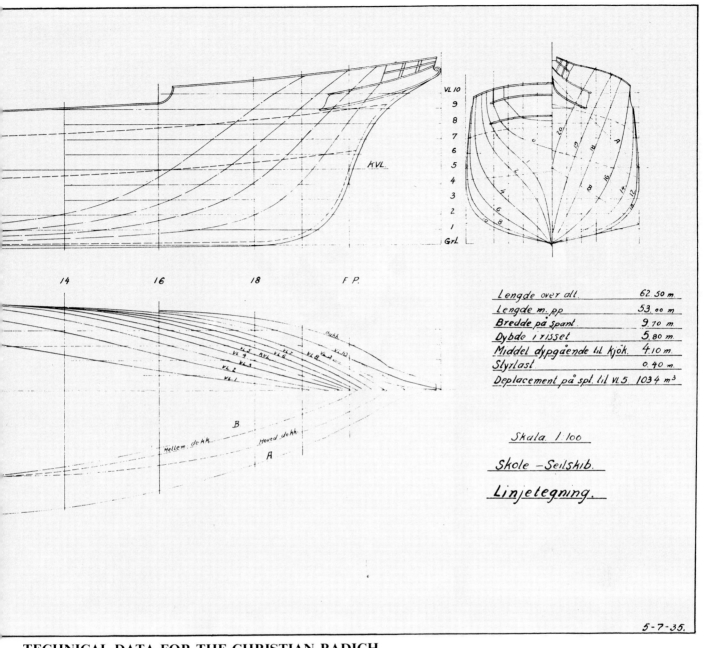

Lengde over alt.   62.50 m.
Lengde m. pp   53.00 m.
Bredde på spant.   9.70 m.
Dybde i risset   5.80 m.
Middel dypgående til kjøk.   4.10 m.
Styrlast   0.40 m.
Deplacement på spt. til VL 5 1034 m³

Skala. 1:100

Skole — Seilskib.

Linjetegning.

5-7-35.

TECHNICAL DATA FOR THE CHRISTIAN RADICH

LOA: (length above deck, overall length):	204.0 feet	62.0 meters
LWL: (length at waterline):	174.0 feet	53.0 meters
BEAM:	32.0 feet	9.7 meters
DRAFT:	15.5 feet	4.5 meters
DISPLACEMENT:	1,034 tons	
GROSS TONNAGE:	676 tons	
RIGGING: 3 masts, 27 sails	greatest height, 128.0 feet	
SAIL AREA:	1,350 m²	
MOTOR: 12 cyl., 2-stroke GM diesel, 2 power plants, each 109 kw.	650 horsepower	

The large white swan and some smaller ones.
PHOTOGRAPH: HARALD TUSBERG

After an eventful day· it's easy to fall asleep before you're in your bunk . . .

CONTENTS PREFACE

    I Prelude in Hommelvik   9
   II 88 Young Boys Come Aboard   12
  III The Race to Tenerife   22
   IV The Northeast Trade Wind – That Disappeared   30
    V The Battle of Bermuda   35
   VI Second Place Overall   42
  VII Magnificent Days in New York   50
 VIII Journey to the Great Lakes   61
   IX We Meet the People around the Lakes   67
    X The Mass Media Accompany the Ship   76
   XI Out to Sea Again   86
  XII Homeward Bound   91
 XIII The Hurricane   100
  XIV Thanks for Our Summer Together, Boys!   115
      Postscript   118
      History of the Ship   121
      Technical Data for the *Christian Radich*   127

128

main-royal

mizzen-royal

main-topgallant

mizzen-topgallant

mizzen-royal staysail

upper main-topsail

upper mizzen-topsail

mizzen-topgallant
staysail

lower main-topsail

lower mizzen-topsail

spanker

crossjack

mizzen-topmast staysail

mainsail